THE GOSPEL FOR THE CLOCKAHOLIC

THOMAS L. ARE

Y0-ELA-052

8-18-'89

Joanna and glory spirits

Judson Press® Valley Forge

THE GOSPEL FOR THE CLOCKAHOLIC

Copyright © 1985
Judson Press, Valley Forge, PA 19482-0851

All rights reserved. No part of this publication may be reproduced, stored in a retrievial system, or transmitted in any form or by any means, electronic, mechanical, photocopying, recording, or otherwise, without the prior permission of the copyright owner, except for brief quotations included in a review of the book.
The Scripture quotations in this publication are from the Revised Standard Version of the Bible copyrighted 1946, 1952 © 1971, 1973 by the Division of Christian Education of the National Council of the Churches of Christ in the U.S.A., and used by permission.

Library of Congress Cataloging in Publication Data

Are, Thomas L., 1932-
    The Gospel for the clockaholic.
        1. Time management—Religious aspects—Christianity.
I. Title.
BV4598.5.A74   1985   640'.43   84-23339
ISBN 0-8170-1075-0

The name JUDSON PRESS is registered as a trademark in the U.S. Patent Office. Printed in the U.S.A. ⊕

Dedicated to
LOUISE WALLACE
who organizes my time.

Contents

Introduction

"This will only take a moment," the doctor said, "but it's going to hurt a bit."

As he probed my knee, I gripped the edge of the table and gritted my teeth. *Hurry*, I thought. *I can't stand it much longer.*

"About through," he said.

It seemed like an hour to me; in reality it had been less than a minute.

Three days later I visited my daughter, Martha, at college. We spent the entire afternoon together as she showed me her favorite places on campus. I listened to her talk, watched her laugh, and I realized how much I enjoyed being with her. Then, all too soon, our time was up. "Gotta' go now," she said, "it was a good day,"

"Hard to believe it's so late," I said. "Seemed like ten minutes."

"Yeah, when you're having fun, time flies."

Driving home, I compared my time with the doctor and my time with Martha and I thought. *Funny thing about time. Sometimes a long time seems short and a short time seems long. I guess the difference is in quality. The more quality of the time, the less I'm aware of its passing.*

An entire afternoon with Martha seemed like a moment. It was wonderfully pleasant, but its swift passing frightened me.

I felt the anxiety that comes with the awareness of time running out. Children grow up, jobs change, friends move away, and death comes. In time, everything passes away. With life so short, I don't want to waste a moment of it.

I remember Mr. Lewis, a friend of my childhood. "Yes sir," he declared, "time's the one thing we all got the same of. Them folks rushing around out there ain't gonna catch a bit o'it. When a minute's gone, it's gone forever." Mr. Lewis worked as the delivery man for a small family-owned grocery store. For a person with little formal education, Mr. Lewis impressed my child's mind as the smartest man in the world.

"All's gonna be gone 'fore you know it," he would say. "Might as well slow up and enjoy a bit of it while you got it."

Every time Mr. Lewis made a delivery, he helped me to analyze life, but nothing influenced me more than his respect for time. I've struggled with clock pressure all my days and probably always will. But along the way I have learned some ways to reduce its stress.

Therefore, when I was asked to write a book on time management, I jumped at the opportunity.

Immediately I checked the library shelves to see what had already been written. I found at least twenty books on time management, each one saying essentially the same thing and all of them designed *to make us more time conscious.*

Of all the writers, experts, seminar leaders, and college professors who wrote about time management, none spoke of becoming *less* aware of time. That's what I'm writing about.

I will deal with quality time.

The Bible uses two words for time. The first is *chronos,* which refers to linear time, that which is measured by the clock and calendar. Most time management books deal with this kind of time.

The Bible also speaks of another kind of time. *Kairos* refers to God-filled, or quality time. When a child says, "We had to wait in line for half an hour," he speaks of *chronos.* When he says, "I had the best time of my life," he speaks of *kairos*.

We all hunger for quality time. But if we're not careful, we can prevent it from happening. An addiction to *chronos* can crowd out *kairos*. We become so busy *doing*, we take no opportunity to *be*.

If you are one of those few laid-back, easygoing people who seldom feels hostility and often enjoys listening to others, you don't need this book. If you never feel rushed and if you like the person you have become in the last few years, you can stop reading right now. You can go write your own book, for you know something most of us have missed.

If you have already grown impatient with the slow pace of reading this book and you are thinking of two other things you should be doing right now, then this book may help you. If in the past few weeks you've lost your temper, yelled at the careless driver in front of you, cluttered your desk with more than a month's work and been too busy to pray, then let me tell you about George.

George is a "clockaholic." His addiction to the clock has squeezed most of the quality out of his life. But he can get quality time back. And so can you.

1   Run, George, Run

"**6**:10. Oh, no! I've overslept again."

George threw the covers aside and rushed to the bathroom. Seven minutes later he was looking for his belt—the slim one that fit the loops of his blue trousers. George seldom ate breakfast, but he usually took time to enjoy a quick cup of coffee. Not today. He had to make up ten minutes of lost time.

In the car backing out, George noticed the gas needle pointing close to "Empty." He leaned over for a closer look. He thought, *a little space before the needle reaches "Empty." No time to stop for gas now.* If he didn't beat the traffic to the expressway, he'd never get to town. He would have to chance it. On the other hand, it would be terrible to give out on the cloverleaf in the middle of rush hour.

"Damn," he said out loud. "What a way to start the day!"

"Wouldn't you know it," he sighed, as though someone else were listening as he drove beside the other cars on the highway. "Don't stop now. Just keep on moving."

"Move," he said to the car ahead of him. But there was nowhere to go. Traffic jammed up all three lanes. "Oh, God," he prayed, "don't let me run out of gas here."

Twenty-two minutes later George entered his office. In spite of the slow start, he arrived a few minutes ahead of schedule.

It's a good thing, he thought, looking at all the papers piled up on his desk.

He looked over the first business letter, then a second, then back to the first. Before finishing, his mind raced ahead to another project. George had vaulted into his daily race.

George normally thinks of more than one task at a time and seldom finishes one before starting another. Sometimes he outruns life. He sets deadlines. "I'll get all of it done before five, if it kills me," he said. On some days, he does get all of it done.

On the way home George checked his list again. It had been a good day. Almost everything needing attention had been at least touched. A few things to be carried over until tomorrow but, all in all, it had been a productive day.

"Gas," he said. "Gotta get gas." George pulled up to the self-service pumps and put the hose in the tank. *These pumps are so slow. It takes forever,* he thought.

About that time, the attendant asked, "How are you?"

"Oh, fine," George said, "Nearly gave out this morning on the expressway. Got caught behind a fender bender. You know, if someone could invent a way to get to town without having to fight traffic!"

"Yeah," said the attendant.

George went on talking. For almost five minutes he talked, explaining his entire day to a teenage boy who had simply asked, "How are you?"

Gonna' be late getting home, George thought. *Oh, well, that's the story of my life.*

After supper he cleaned up loose ends. Three phone calls and two hours of work from the briefcase and finally George told his wife, "I'm quitting now. Just too tired to do any more."

"You are still planning for us to go out with the Frys Thursday night?" she asked.

"Oh, honey. I'm so tired by the time I get home, I don't want to go out with anyone. Couldn't we just stay home one night?"

Later, before falling asleep, George reflected on his day. *I just don't have enough time. Maybe I should attend one of those Time Management Seminars and get myself organized.*

Two weeks later, George invested three days and $265 to have an expert tell him how to save time.

"Master your time and master your life," the leader said. "Your goal is to get everything done in the shortest length of time with the fewest wasted motions. Here are the rules."

Never waste a minute. He could even make use of the three minutes in the dentist chair waiting for the Novocain to take effect, but he must plan for it. Carry a book or outline a project.

Avoid interruptions. He learned how to cut people off and not waste time talking about things that didn't interest him. He especially thought it clever to cut off a long-winded phone caller by pressing the button while "you are talking," as the leader had said. That way the caller would think the phone company messed up. After all, who cuts himself off?

Make a "to-do" list. Identify the one-minute projects, the three-minute projects, the ten-, thirty-, and so forth. All during the day George checked off each project as he completed it.

Review. Stop at the end of each day, week, month, and year to see if he accomplished his goals.

In short, be more time conscious.

George remembered these rules well!

George got his money's worth. He began checking his watch every few minutes before the seminar even got started. By the time he graduated, he was a full-blown clockaholic. So much to do and so little time in which to do it.

George thought he had become the master of his time. In reality, he had become its slave.

Remember the story of *Gulliver's Travels?* The king sent forth investigators. They were to unmask any dangerous items that the giant Gulliver might use against them. Sure enough, they found a great engine that made noise like a waterfall. It had an invisible partition that protected the figures on its face.

The king's sleuths had found Gulliver's watch. In reporting to the king, they said it must be Gulliver's god because he consulted it so often.

They could have been describing George. He checks his watch a hundred times a day. Even though he just looked at it, when someone asks "What time is it?" he has to look again. Worse still, if it's later than he expected, George feels guilty. "Time is life," he said. "Waste time and you throw away your life."

George works so hard at managing his time, he reminds me of the family who recently installed a sophisticated burglar alarm system.

Every time they come home, the first thing they do is check the system. They punch the right codes to disarm it before entering the house. Every member of the family carries a little keyboard on his or her person to signal any disorder. Before going to bed, the system must be programmed. First thing in the morning, they set it again, and it must be armed as they leave the house for work. Six times each day their burglar alarm system demands attention.

Their entire life centers on the burglar alarm. Nothing seems to dominate their minds like the fear of being robbed.

In the same way, George is addicted to the clock. He's caught in a trap. He concentrates on time in order to be free of it, but the more attention he gives it, the more it dominates him.

George also reminds me of my friend Marvin, who is equally compulsive but in a different way.

Marvin majors in learning names. He consistently memorizes the name of everyone who enters a room. One night at a party, he successfully called by name over one hundred guests whom he had never previously known. "Names are important," Marvin said. "People appreciate anyone who remembers their names." But Marvin works so hard at recalling names that he hardly notices anything else. Rather than feeling that Marvin is friendly, most people see him as somewhat entertaining and terribly preoccupied. His commitment to learning names destroys his purpose for doing it.

Both Marvin and George work from a private agenda which makes it difficult for their friends to relax around them.

George wonders why he feels strained in his relationships with other people when he works so hard. One night he arrived for a committee meeting at the church precisely on time, seven-thirty sharp. He looked around but saw no one else, not even the cars of the other members. Something was wrong. The entire committee wouldn't be late. Then it struck him as he looked at the dark building. The meeting was not until eight o'clock. How could he have made such a stupid mistake? What was he going to do for thirty minutes? Not enough time to go home, and too dark to read. All George could do was wait. Again he checked his watch, thirty-six minutes past seven.

Twenty-minutes later, other committee members arrived. "Where have you guys been? I've been waiting since seven-thirty." The fact that George had been responsible for his own mistake seemed to have slipped his mind. "Let's go," he said, with an edge on his voice.

"Take it easy, George. Let's wait for the others," Lib said as they sat around the table.

"Well, they should be here."

As the meeting started, George presented his plans that the church hire someone part-time to begin a new ministry to singles. "We can get someone for $300 a month and you know how many singles we have in our church."

"I don't know," Lib said slowly. "Just what will this new person do?"

"Well, he'll. . . . Why are you so opposed to this, Lib?"

"I'm not opposed to anything," Lib said. "I just want to know more about it."

"There's not much more to know. We'll hire somebody to do singles ministry and let him or her decide what to do. I move we approve the money," George said.

He lost the vote, and after several more verbal exchanges, George also lost the respect of the committee. He had done his homework and come to the meeting with a good plan but he had sacrificed it to his own time anxiety and hostility.

George never wastes time without feeling guilty, and he projects that anxiety on those around him.

By now, George has become a chronic clockaholic. If he doesn't change, chances are it will kill him.

George would hardly admit harboring a concern for his own death but the fear of dying influences his lifestyle. "One world at a time," he's quick to quote. But in reality, he knows that someday he is going to die. If that were not so, he would have all the time in the world. George never puts together those parts: the fear of death and his rush through life, but combined, they team up against him. The feeling that there's so much to do and so little time to do it in shortens his time. The thought of changing his lifestyle now to avoid jeopardizing his health ten years hence seems like a poor bargain. After all, opportunities to succeed only come along once in a lifetime. He'll seize every opportunity now and will deal with death later.

Yet, there is more and more evidence that George will never live until later. According to Philip Goldberg,[1] coronary disease in America has increased 500 percent in the last fifty years. A million Americans have heart attacks each year. Sixty-five percent of these victims—die!

Approximately twenty-five million Americans have hypertension (high blood pressure) causing an additional sixty thousand deaths. Eight million Americans have ulcers, adding ten thousand deaths every year. Twelve million are alcoholics. Ten million are diabetics.

Americans consume sixteen thousand tons of aspirin each year, at a cost of five hundred million dollars. More than two hundred and thirty million prescriptions are filled each year, including five billion tranquilizers.

Of American males now forty-five years of age, 10 percent

[1] Philip Goldberg, *Executive Health* (New York: McGraw-Hill Publications Inc., 1979), p. 19-20.

will not make it to fifty-five. George will probably be one of them.

Perhaps no one has described George better than two San Francisco cardiologists, Meyer Friedman and Ray Rosenman. These doctors began investigating the relationship between stress behavior and heart disease twenty-five years ago. They conclude that "Type A's," those with a chronic sense of time urgency and excessive competitive drive have seven times the incidence of coronary disease than the "Type B's" who are more relaxed.

Many medical experts identify the leading cause of "Type-A" deaths, not as diet, exercise, or nicotine, but as a time-pressured lifestyle.

But even if George does survive and lives to be one hundred years old, his clockaholic personality will constantly rob him of most of the quality times of his life. The pressure and hostility he feels each day may classify him as surviving, but hardly living.

"It's a competitive jungle out there," George told his family. "You have to knock yourself out every minute, just to keep up."

I understand George. I am a competitor myself. I grew up believing that I was a nobody, a no-good sinner. On a scale of one to ten, I ranked a zero. "You'll have to work hard," they told me, "ever to amount to anything." Like George, I grew up determined to prove that I could come out on top.

Soon I joined the adult rat race. *Climb on the backs of others if you must,* I thought, *but get ahead.* I was subtle. Most of all, I would never have admitted how desperately I needed to *be somebody.*

Had I been with the disciples that day on the road to Capernaum, I also would have argued over "who was the greatest" (Mark 9:34).

Remember that day Jesus asked them what they were talking about among themselves. They became silent. They were ashamed. None of them wanted to admit his need to be important.

It amazes me that Jesus did not condemn them for their arrogance. He understood human nature and recognized that just as we have a need for air and food, we also hunger for significance. We all want our lives to matter. Jesus said that we go about it the wrong way. Rather than killing ourselves being competitive, he said, "If anyone would be first, he must be last of all and servant of all" (Mark 9:35).

After thirty years of adult life, I am learning to trust Jesus. He loves me because of who I am, not because I have become "king of the mountain." I have also learned that the best feelings I have about myself come when I take the time to help someone else up the ladder.

George, on the other hand, hears the words of Jesus like a contradiction. Last cannot be first. George is determined to come out ahead of his "competitors" if it's the last thing he does.

George is a chronic clockaholic and it's slowly killing him, physically and emotionally. While he probably cannot totally change his basic personality, he can modify his lifestyle toward more meaning and less stress.

2   Caught in Chronos

"**I** know you have to work on your income tax tonight, but . . ."

"But what?" George asked, smiling at his wife, Doris.

"But I need you to check the lock on the door downstairs," Doris replied. "It won't take a minute."

George needed at least four hours to prepare his taxes. He also wanted to repair the door. Or maybe he wanted to delay the burden of tax work. At any rate, he spent over an hour doing home repairs.

At 9:10, George spread tax forms out on the table. He plugged in the calculator and started shuffling checks.

"Daddy," Phillip said, coming into the room. "Can you come to my ball game tomorrow night?"

"I don't know, son. If I don't get on this tax work, I'll be right here tomorrow night."

"We only have one more game after tomorrow. But if you can't make it, I'll understand."

"I'll try! That's the best I can say, son," George snapped.

As Phillip backed out of the room, George questioned his own anger. Why had Phil irritated him? He had made a reasonable request. Yet, his "understanding" disturbed George. How could he understand the pressure George felt? There's just not enough time to do everything, he thought, trying to defend his guilt feelings.

George spent the rest of the night working on his taxes. But he was interrupted a few more times. Someone from the church called and asked him to work six nights on the special stewardship program.

"Six nights? That's too much time." George turned him down.

Then a magazine salesman called and tied him up for four minutes. George said no, but the irritation caused by the interruption upset him for the rest of the night.

What a way to spend an evening, George thought. He had only one task to accomplish and had hardly gotten started on it. Most of the night he had spent doing things he really didn't want to do.

There is no way out for him. As long as George is a husband, father, breadwinner, churchgoer, taxpayer, citizen, and businessman, he will be called upon to do numerous things he really doesn't want to do. He will juggle his schedule over and over again for the sake of others.

As a company man, he gives the bigger part of every working day to his employers, where George feels every minute should be accounted for. He is obsessed with time measurement. He has three clocks in his office, two in his bedroom and den, one in his car; and he wears a watch guaranteed to be accurate within one second per month.

He can justify the passing of time only if he has something to show for it.

George is caught in *chronos*, the relentless passing of time. He spends hour after hour doing the things that must be done. Mostly, he hates it.

He needs *kairos*, those experiences packed with meaning and adventure. But he's so busy doing the mundane, there's no time left for the meaningful. If only he could make his time count.

Kairos, as far as I know, never happens apart from *chronos*.

It's not as though we are caught in a battle between two enemies. Special times grow out of the ordinary and, whether planned or not, the precious moments usually catch us by surprise.

In the midst of a *kairos* experience, *chronos* time keeps ticking. But in the midst of a quality experience, we don't notice the clock as much.

In the famous parable, the Samaritan had his God-filled experience. All Christendom honors the love he expressed in helping the wounded man in the ditch. Jesus called him good because of his quality moment.

We overlook the fact that he probably worked many ordinary hours to earn the money he gave the innkeeper. His God-charged opportunity grew out of his everyday *chronos* responsibility. Along the way of his regular day's work, the Samaritan stumbled onto a *kairos* opportunity.

Perhaps that's the way it comes to each of us. We busy ourselves doing the ordinary things expected of us, even things we don't enjoy doing. Then, at an unexpected moment, we recognize a point in time *touched by God.*

I heard the story of a businessman rushing to catch the subway. As he raced for the train door, a small boy stepped in his way. They collided. Pieces of the boy's jigsaw puzzle flew all over the platform. The man looked at the train. There would be only a few seconds before the doors would shut and the train pull away. He took a few swift steps, then stopped. He looked at the bewildered boy and slowly walked back. Much to the boy's amazement, the man put down his briefcase and began picking up pieces of the boy's puzzle. Together they searched and gathered every piece back into the box. Then they sat down and waited for the next train.

As the man boarded the train, the boy reached out and grabbed his sleeve. "Mister," he said, "Are you Jesus?"

For a moment, as the train pulled away, the man felt that maybe—he was.

In a time of *chronos*, he had experienced an unexpected moment of *kairos*.

On the other hand, sometimes *kairos* moments are planned.

I visited my mother on her seventy-third birthday. Late that night she showed me a picture of the old farmhouse where she had been born. "We moved away when I was fifteen," she said. "And I've never been back. I wonder if it's still there."

"Let's go see," I said. It was hard to believe that my mother had lived a hundred miles from her childhood home for half a century and had never been back.

"I'm not sure we can even find it," she said, "We lived about seven miles out of town."

"We'll go see."

Three hours later we were driving seven miles out each road from town.

Suddenly, "There it is. . . . That's it. . . . It looks. . . . Oh, that's our house," she squealed.

No one was home but we walked around the house. She touched the big oak tree out front, sat on the porch, and told me a dozen childhood stories about growing up with eight brothers and sisters.

"There used to be a swimming hole on the other side of this field," she said. We walked together until we found it. We also found the old family cemetery. She identified half the grave markers.

She pointed to the grave of Sarah. "We took her into our home because she had been burned. People in the city wouldn't accept her because her face was scarred. But with us," my mother said, "she was just family."

Then we saw the grave of a three-year-old girl. "She died in our house, too. She drank some lye when her father butchered a hog. We all stayed awake for three days praying for her."

"No one ever got sick without your grandmother being there," my mother said.

"Your parents were good folks, weren't they?" I asked, for I had never known my grandparents.

"We attended worship, Sunday school, church picnics and took part in every mission project known to the church. My mother wore out the seats of our clothes with so much sitting in church. When we didn't have enough to buy shoes, we still tithed our money."

All that day I visualized my roots as never before as I listened to stories of my mother's childhood. As she told me of my grandparents, I learned something about myself. I may never live up to all that heritage, but I'll never quite be free of its influence either.

That day spent with my mother at her childhood home was all too short. It still stands out as one of the richest experiences of my life. I planned the day but the quality of it took me by surprise. The rewards were more than well worth the investment of my time. Neither of us was conscious of the passing of time until it was over. Unlike George, I believe a *kairos* experience is always worth the *chronos* investment. I don't know how much an hour of time is worth but I'm convinced that time in itself, without quality, is overvalued. On the other hand, quality time is priceless.

Time defies description. Time is easier to measure than to define. Saint Augustine pondered the mystery of it and confessed, "I know well enough what it is, provided that nobody asks me; but if I am asked what it is and try to explain, I am baffled."[1] But no undefinable commodity ever received more attention than time. Books and plans to seize it, to escape it, to kill it, or to fill it, flood our lives. Some preachers declare that time is God's gift and to waste a moment of it is a grievous sin.

George would agree. "The clock is always ticking," he said. "The greatest challenge we face today is to stop wasting time. We could be 30, maybe even 40 percent more productive if we valued time."

I half agree with George. Time is precious and should not be wasted. I want to save time, but not in order to *have* more

[1] Augustine, *Confessions* XI, 14.

time. What would be the point? Instead, I want to manage time to have more quality experiences. In other words, exchange *chronos* for *kairos*, not *chronos* for *chronos*.

Neither do I see time as an enemy to be conquered. We really can't manipulate time, even for a good cause. Our effort to have more of it by controlling it breaks down and defeats itself. Therefore our *motive* for managing time makes the difference, even when the management looks the same.

I remember coming home one day several years ago feeling a need to make amends with my nine-year-old son. I had neglected him recently and felt guilty.

That afternoon I had seen in the store a wallet-size calculator. I'll buy this for Jimmy, I thought. It'll prove to him what a super dad I am. The rest of that day I could hardly wait to go home.

"Look, Jim, look what I brought you," I called to him as I got out of the car. Jim ran to me, excited. Both of us grinned as Jim opened the package. Then his expression changed.

"A calculator?" he said.

"I thought you'd like one."

"Oh, Dad, I don't need a calculator. I already have one better than this." He dropped it on the car seat and ran back to play with his friend.

I stood there stunned and angry. *The ungrateful kid,* I thought. I had paid twelve dollars for that calculator.

Later that night, as I thought it over, I realized that I had bought the calculator out of my own need, not for Jim. I was giving it to him to buy his reaction. On the way home I had already pictured how Jim was going to react to his gift. "Gee, Dad, a calculator. Just what I always wanted."

When Jim didn't give me what I had paid for, I was furious.

On the other hand, if I had been thinking of Jim rather than of myself, I may or may not have bought a calculator. But I would have given it to meet Jim's needs, not mine.

Bringing home a calculator may have looked the same to an outsider. But *the motive* for buying it made all the difference in what it meant to me.

I believe the same thing about time management. If the motive is to *get more done in a shorter length of time, it only adds pressure.* The time we save only confines us. On the other hand, managing time to be available for quality experiences frees us.

I may see time as some mysterious influence in my life to be pushed and squeezed for all it's worth. Or I may choose by faith to see time as God's precious gift to me. How I live in it may look the same to an outsider. I still go to work everyday and try not to waste a minute of time. My motive in the use of time makes all the difference in the world to me.

God and I are partners in time. As someone has said, every new day is God's gift to me. How I use that day is my gift to God. My schedule looks a lot like George's. Yet I use time as an opportune friend, an expression of the presence of God. George seems only to be driven by time as by an enemy.

We are all caught in *chronos,* but we can make it a friend to serve us. Our health and happiness depend on it.

3   Dying to Be First

"The Lord giveth and the Lord taketh . . ." the minister
was saying, but George hardly heard it. People crowded every
pew; friends, business associates, even competitors. There
must have been six hundred people there for Stan's funeral.
Everybody respected Stan, and he would be missed. He had
practically run the company.

They deserved to miss Stan, George thought. *No one really
appreciated him while he was alive. Maybe now they'd realize
how much Stan did for them.* George knew he would certainly
miss him. Stan had been his friend since college days.

As George was sitting in church, absorbing the sights and
sounds of the funeral, he identified with Stan. "It's unfair,"
he whispered to his wife sitting next to him. "Stan was the
best of 'em."

As they followed the coffin down the aisle after the service,
George was aware for the first time of how much anger he
felt. Or maybe he felt mostly shock. Stan had been in perfect
health. He had given up smoking ten years ago, jogged six
miles almost every day, and watched his diet. He worked hard,
loved his family, gave money to his church, and was one of
the most productive men in the business. Stan was on his way.
Then WHAM, without warning. A heart attack. While jog-

ging, of all things! *Exercise was supposed to prevent heart attacks,* George thought.

Most people are under the impression that diet, exercise and staying free of cigarettes provides the best possible insurance against heart attack. Not necessarily so, according to some leading cardiologists, if these restraints do not also include stress control.

Friedman and Rosenman in their book *Type A Behavior and Your Heart* point to *personality patterns as the leading cause of heart disease.* They feel that it's not diet, heredity or smoking, but primarily a person's behavior patterns that decide whether or not he will be stricken. In a study of 3,500 men, thirty-five to sixty years old, they found that Type A, compulsive, fast-driving men had three times the incidence of heart disease than easy-going men.

> Type A behavior, according to these physicians, leads to an excess discharge of the so-called stress hormones—cortisol, epinephrine, and norepinephrine. Type A's produce an excess of insulin in their blood and take three to four times longer to rid their body of dietary cholesterol after each meal. These changes, they explain, can lead to the narrowing of blood vessels and increased deposits of clotting elements in the blood.[1]
>
> In the absence of the Type A behavior pattern, coronary heart disease almost never occurs before seventy years of age, regardless of the fatty foods eaten, the cigarettes smoked, or the lack of exercise. But when this behavior pattern is present, coronary disease can easily erupt in one's thirties or forties.[2]

Who Is the "Type A"?

They list the main characteristics of the Type A person as: (1) sense of time urgency (those having "hurry sickness," always trying to stuff more into less time); (2) quest for the achievement of increased numbers of things; (3) insecurity of status in spite of outward appearance of confidence; and (4) hostility which grows out of competition.

What Friedman and Rosenman say in this revealing book

[1]Philip Goldberg, *Executive Health* (New York: McGraw-Hill Inc., 1979), p. 103.
[2]Meyer Friedman and Ray H. Rosenman, *Type A Behavior & Your Heart* (New York: Alfred A. Knopf, Inc., 1974), p. 9.

is that a healthy personality is vital to a healthy heart.

They do not minimize the known killers; smoking, heredity, cholesterol, and so forth, but say that these factors become most dangerous when influenced by Type A behavior.

They point out that the cholesterol level of accountants rises as the tax deadline of April fifteenth approaches.

In Japan the incidence of heart disease has quadrupled since World War II as that nation adopted American patterns of conduct.

On the other hand, Navajo Indians consume more cholesterol than Caucasians but rarely suffer heart attacks. The Masai tribesman of Kenya, who consume frighteningly huge amounts of cholesterol and animal fat, never suffer from coronary heart disease.

The Harvard School of Nutrition reports a study of 579 sets of Irish brothers, one of each set living in Boston and the other in Ireland. Heart attacks in the American brothers were twice that of their homeland brothers. Yet they all had similar eating, exercise, and smoking habits.

Fifty years ago, during the Depression, coronary deaths doubled in four years. Dr. Flanders Dunbar at Columbia Presbyterian Medical Center at New York studied some sixteen hundred patients with hypertension, heart disease, and diabetes. She labeled heart attacks as "a middle-age disease" found mostly in "self-made men. Their overriding personality trait she describes as 'compulsive striving.' They would rather die than fail."[3]

Heart attacks in America have multiplied five times in the past fifty years in spite of the fact that cholesterol intake and smoking have not increased at the same rate. The thing that has increased is pace.

No one says that bad eating habits, lack of exercise, and cigarette smoking are not harmful. In fact, these risk factors feed upon each other. Stress can increase the desire for cigarette smoking,.which in return causes high blood pressure, elevates

[3] Flanders Dunbar as quoted in Walter McQuade and Ann Aikman, *Stress*, (New York: Bantam Books, Inc., 1974), pp. 31-32.

cholesterol levels, and causes more stress. Such a cycle can be deadly. But these physical abuses alone will probably not kill you unless you are a Type A personality—like George.

In those rare occasions when George allows himself to think about his life span, he feels concern. Most of all, he is aware that his own father died of a heart attack at age fifty-three.

"You've got to be careful," the doctor said to George three years ago while giving him a physical examination. "I'm convinced that how long your parents lived is a major indication of your potential life span."

"What do you mean 'be careful'?" George asked.

"Watch your blood pressure and get plenty of exercise."

Since that time, George jogs religiously. He feels great satisfaction that he can now run further and with less effort than many men half his age. Early in the morning, late evening, hot or cold, at home or off on a business trip, George jogs. He races against himself to see if he can shave off a minute or make an extra block or two. George actually turns his recreation time into a race against the clock.

He could do worse than jog. He could play handball or tennis which would pit him against someone else. His competitive spirit would drive him to achieve even more. "Keeps my heart pumping like it should," he would say.

Yet, "approximately two hundred thousand American men who had never experienced a single symptom of coronary heart disease died suddenly last year. More than a third of them died during, or a few minutes after, indulging in strenuous activity."[4]

Exercise influences the muscular element of the heart, but it cannot prevent the arteries from narrowing. George would do better to work toward changing his lifestyle than to count on jogging by itself to keep him healthy.

It's possible that George has inherited from his father a *clock-racing personality* rather than a weak heart. He constantly struggles against an unknown force that drives him to

[4]Friedman, *Type A Behavior*, p. 182.

live like his dad. George operates out of a compulsion to be more successful than Dad, at a much earlier age.

"Remember," George says, "the early bird gets the worm." He believes that his efforts to get the report in first will reward him with a promotion.

Yet there is a fundamental flaw in George's logic. He struggles with an anxiety that cannot be relieved by material success. On the conscious level, George seldom thinks about his father's death; but every year he clicks off another anniversary. He has already lived two years beyond Dad and he carries around an unacknowledged fear. "Who, me?" he would say. "I'm not afraid to die. I just don't want to die right now. There's so much to do and I'm just getting started." The closest George will come to dealing with his own death anxiety is to think of it in terms of working time. "My father died young," he once told a friend. "So I may have less time than most to get things set up for my family."

If George knew why he chose to overdrive himself, he would discover that it has little to do with concern for his family, or anyone else. It's not that George is selfish. He hides in work because of a subconscious fear of early death. "Security," he said, "comes from success, success comes from accomplishments." He cannot let up, even when he tries.

"I need some time off," George announced to his wife. "Let's take a few days, go up and visit Paul and just relax." *It is so unlike George to schedule rest time, he must really be tired,* his wife thought.

A week later they left early in the morning to drive across two states to visit an old college friend.

"WOW!" George said as they began dinner. 'Business must be good."

"We've been blessed," Paul replied. "You know how it is."

George looked around at the opulent furnishings in Paul's house. He had noticed the two automobiles and boat as they drove up. "Paul must really be in the money," he whispered to his wife.

George and Paul laughed until midnight, telling stories of their college days. "Remember when so and so . . . ," they said over and over as they talked about each classmate in turn, who married whom, and who now is most successful.

"Too bad about Stan," Paul said, "but that's the way to go."

"Yeah," George said softly, "he was a good man."

"Guess he lived a full life at that," Paul added.

Later that night George tossed in the bed. He was tired from the long day and eight-hour drive but he couldn't fall asleep. Emotions were flying around inside and George couldn't slow up, even when wanting to sleep. Stan's death bothered him. Maybe he had lived a full life, but George wanted more. It could have happened to him. He felt guilty for feeling relief that it was Stan and not him.

Stan's death was not what George identified as disturbing him most that night. He focused more on Paul's obvious success. George had worked hard and by comparison had done much better than most of his friends, but he was not satisfied. He envied Paul, and he wanted it the other way around; he would choose to have Paul envy him.

Next morning, after a swim in the family pool, Paul suggested a game of tennis.

"I'm out of shape," George said. "Haven't played in years, but you're on."

George played hard, but he lost. He got upset. He blamed the sun, the wind, the weight of his racket, and Paul's dirty shots as the reasons for his loss. "Let's quit," he said, walking off the court. "Besides, I've got to phone the office." Ten minutes later, George decided to go home.

"But George," his wife said, "I thought we were going to stay three days."

"I know, honey. I've got to get back to the office. Something's come up. If we leave by two, we'll get home by ten."

Eight o'clock the next morning George entered his office, tired. He had driven several hundred miles and hardly slept at all. He felt better now. He was back at work—in his own element. His visit to Paul had been worth it, George thought. Made him more determined. If Paul could do it, George could do it. *Wonder what a swimming pool like that costs?* he thought.

George has no idea what he has done to himself. Something from within had called out for rest. He planned for a few days of quality time. He had exposed himself to one of his deepest needs: to relax and share with a friend his concerns about life and death. Then he sacrificed it to his own lack of self-esteem.

George tries to overcome his insecurity by establishing an impressive track record. He thinks that if he can do something spectacular, it will add to his feeling of significance. So George works to accomplish. Unfortunately, all his compulsive efforts to produce add mostly to his blood pressure and leave him tired. Worse than that, they destroy the best hope he has of feeling a sense of security and self-worth. George doesn't know it, but his great success image destroys the relationships he desperately needs.

George can know his value as a person only through loving others—not by owning a big house, even one with a swimming pool.

"George," his colleague Eddie said, "what are you doing here? I didn't think you were going to be back 'til Monday."

"Couldn't help it," George responded. "Duty calls."

"Oh, come on, George, surely it could have waited until Monday. You don't take enough time off."

"Can't afford to. If you had to pay the kind of income taxes I do, you'd know what I mean."

"Guess so," Eddie said as he turned to walk away. *It's hard to get close to that guy,* he thought. Eddie made a mental note to talk to his wife about having some friends over one night for hamburgers. But he felt sure George wouldn't be one of them.

No wonder Eddie chose to get away from George. Whether he realized it or not, Eddie had been put down. George's complaint about taxes he had to pay was a subtle way of bragging about how much money he had made. Eddie's expression of concern got lost in George's choice to present himself secure.

George measures every relationship on the scale of successes, and he constantly competes. He ranks himself behind Paul and ahead of Eddie. But he shares no real friendship with either one. Just as well, he thinks, he has so much to do. At least busyness covers his anxiety.

I understand George. I have never suffered from heart disease, ulcers, diabetes, allergies, or many of the other stress-related diseases, but I have had horrible migraines. For ten years, periodically, most often hitting on Monday mornings, one side of my head felt as though it would split open.

My migraines always came when I was relaxing after a pressure time. It was as though I could handle the stress of any moment. I didn't know what to do with time off. I stayed busy to keep from thinking about myself.

As a child, I lived with the anxiety of death. I had chronic nephritis. Bed rest, penicillin shots, and a strict diet ruled my life. And always I kept in my mind the child's unasked question, "Am I going to die?" Life should be long, like a book of unending pages. I had reason to fear that my book would be closed before I even knew what it was about.

I can learn to avoid other anxiety-producing situations such as war, hunger, even illness. But the threat of death has no solution. Someday I will certainly die. I just don't know when.

I cannot halt the passage of time, but I can order my life to make it richer. Someone said, "If I can't add days to my life, then let me add life to my days." I think we can do both. We can live longer by living better.

I look at Jesus. He lived only thirty-three years. Of those, he spent only three in public ministry. Yet no one in all of history has accomplished more. Many have lived longer but none better.

I try to copy two aspects of his life.

First, Jesus made himself available for others. Luke tells of the blind man who cried out when he heard Jesus "passing by" (Luke 18:37). Jesus stopped to help.

"If you knew this was the last day of your life, Tom, what would you do?" I have been asked.

"I hope I would stop and care for someone." Oh, I still seek to establish myself. I am concerned with career, finances, and reputation. But every now and then I have those moments of insight when I realize that all life is "passing by." I believe my limited days become richer more by serving others than by grasping for position and possessions.

Second, I learn from Jesus that this life is but one stage in eternity.

Sometimes I get so preoccupied with the temporal things that I miss the things eternal. Like George, I admit to no fear of death. I just don't want to die this week. It's the *time* hidden in death that I fear. I don't want to die before I get all my chores done.

Unless I see my life in the midst of "forever," the brevity of my days terrifies me. If Jesus is right, it's not that I will live my life so many days and then enter eternity. Eternity includes now. My physical death will mark the edge of a new adventure, not the end of it.

When I spend all my time and energy on things temporal, I create an emotional stress which actually shortens the length of my days.

I respect this life. I will diet to control cholesterol and I will try to keep nicotine and smoke tar from clogging up my lungs.

I will even exercise, for the human body seems to be the only machine in the world that improves with use.

Most of all, I will work as hard as George. But I will work to *express who I am, not to make me somebody* or to hide from myself. Beethoven wrote music, not for money or recognition, even though he needed both. He composed music to express his inner soul.

That is living, not dying, no matter how short our days.

On the other hand, George is killing himself to come in first. Even if he gets there before he has a heart attack, he may discover that having accomplished it all, he still feels empty, angry—and alone.

4   Homemade Hostility

"**A**ndy, doggone it," George yelled, "you always drop the ice tray!"

George had entered the kitchen just as Andy opened the freezer door. Reaching up, he tugged at the ice tray. Then, zoop, it flew over his head and hit the floor. Swoosh. Ice cubes scattered in every direction.

"Andy, doggone it. . . ." The intensity of his own voice surprised George. He turned and stalked through the den, down the hall and into his bedroom. After slamming the door, he collapsed on the bed. Grateful for a quiet moment, he read the afternoon paper. It had been a rough day.

After glancing at the headlines, George flipped over to the sports page. *Maybe the Braves will make it this year*, he thought. *Gotta get better pitching, though, and. . . .*

Then Andy walked in. Tears ran down his cheeks. His eyes were swollen and red and his hands covered his mouth. "Daddy," he said, in a high-pitched voice.

"What happened, Son?" George reached out, thinking Andy had hurt himself or maybe been stung by a bee.

"Daddy," Andy said again, half-crying, "Daddy, that's the first time I ever dropped the ice tray!"

Andy was right. George realized he had brought a lot of anger home with him that had nothing to do with ice trays.

The morning had started okay. At least this time he got up with the alarm clock sounding and had plenty of gasoline. George clicked off chores ahead of schedule for the first forty minutes at work. Then Marion came in. They exchanged a few words of greeting and Marion turned to leave—at least George thought he was leaving. Instead, he pulled up a chair and sat down.

What now? George thought. *Surely he knows I don't have time for a social visit.*

"Been thinking about moving," Marion said.

"That's nice," George replied, trying to show just enough irritation so that Marion might catch on and leave without feeling offended.

"Kids all gone now, you know. We just don't need that big house anymore. Been thinking about a condo."

"Hurumph," George grunted.

"What do you think? The market too soft?"

"Look, Marion, I don't know. I don't have time to talk about it now."

"Oh . . . well, excuse *me*," Marion said, and he walked out.

George felt Marion's irritation but what else could he do? Marion would have talked all day.

At that point, if anyone had suggested to George that he was angry, he would have denied it. He had merely done what any good businessman would have done. He had cleared his office of an intruder so he could get back to his work.

In the next hour George tried to call Mr. Beasley about a budget matter. He was not in. The batteries in George's calculator flashed weak. He misplaced the Sparks report which had to be finished that day. He knew exactly where he had left it but it was not there. He checked through three drawers, two file cabinets, and shuffled every paper on his desk.

"Betty," he yelled to his secretary. "Do you have the Sparks report?"

"No, I don't," she replied as she continued with her work.

George didn't say anything but he flushed with a moment of irritation that Betty had shown so little concern. He wanted her to pick up the panic in his voice and rush in to help look.

Ten minutes later she did come in. "Are you still looking for that report?"

"Yes," he answered with an edge on his voice. "I'm still looking for that report."

"Maybe you took it home with you."

"No, I didn't 'took it home' with me," he mocked. This time, she couldn't miss the anger in his voice.

"Sorry, I'm just trying to help."

George was sorry too, but he was too upset to say so. "It's impossible to get things done around here when nothing works."

The rest of the day went the same for George. Telephone calls interfered with his concentration, people dropped in to ask questions they could answer themselves, and Eddie had the Sparks report. George had forgotten giving it to him. Finally, George left late for home; red lights, traffic, headache, and George remembered another meeting coming up that night.

Then, he walked in the door and Andy dropped the ice tray.

Later that night, he defended himself.

"Let me tell you what heaven is going to be like for me," George said to Doris. "If I ever get to heaven, I'm going to have a completely clear calendar, with nothing to do all day long. Then I can devote the entire day to interruptions."

"I know," she said, "but I wish you wouldn't get so angry."

"Jesus got angry," he snapped back.

"Yes, but Jesus got angry when the situation hurt *others,* not to defend himself."

"I can't help it," George said. "I'm not Jesus."

"You're sure not," she said. "Sometimes I think you're just going to explode."

George really wants to slow down. The flare-up with Andy and his quibble with Doris embarrassed him. Unless he makes some changes, it will happen again.

In spite of his outward impression of having it made, George lives constantly with the fear of not being accepted. He grew up in a home where God was often mentioned. They told him that God would watch over him, protect him, and hold him close while he slept at night *if* . . . if he made good grades, remembered to speak to important adults, and generally conducted himself in a proper manner. It worked for a while. At least George thought so.

Then he went through a stage when God seemed distant and unreal. Naturally George thought God had forsaken him because he did not deserve God's closeness. So George worked harder.

It may have succeeded. He could have performed well enough to feel God's presence again, except that he had an older sister, Beth. Beth could always outdo George. She never dropped the milk bottle, she talked better on the telephone, and she always seemed to have money in her purse. He could never match Beth, but he tried.

George learned at an early age to be competitive. By the time he graduated from college, he was a veteran antagonist. Never again did he feel God's acceptance or fully trust anyone else's unless he could convince himself that he had earned it.

George needed to slow down. He was tired and seldom got enough sleep. Over and over he promised himself that next week he would do something to take care of himself. By next week the same pressures that drove him to shambles last week force him to break the promise.

"I need a day off," he told a friend. "Sometimes I think I could sleep around the clock." The kind of tired George feels cannot be cured by a day in bed. A sleeping tiger still feels like a tiger when he wakes up.

George could be relieved by delegating some of his work and responsibility to someone else. But George can't do that. He can't risk anyone else receiving part of the credit for getting the job done and he doesn't think anyone can do it as well. Like a martyr, he works and strains to get it all done by himself, and to do it better than anyone else could.

George reminds me of the little boy who rushes in every morning to add stars to a chart on the refrigerator door. "I brushed my teeth, combed my hair, made the bed, picked up my clothes." On and on the list goes. He checks each accomplishment until every blank displays a star. He walks back to his room pleased with himself. He has done all the good things. *Does mother really love me?* he wonders. *I hope she does.* In spite of all his accomplishments, George felt more tired and alone than loved. No wonder he is angry. He paid the price but seldom if ever reaped the rewards. He felt cheated and was convinced that life treated him unfairly.

"Free-floating hostility," the psychologists call it, to describe someone who carries around an inner anger.

"George, can you make an appointment with me today at two o'clock and also be across town at another meeting?" Eddie asked.

"I don't see how I can," George replied, a bit puzzled by the illogical question.

"Well I don't see why not," Eddie said with a chuckle, "you sure did it yesterday."

Then George remembered. He had promised to meet Eddie at two and had forgotten. But he saw nothing to laugh about. George never liked a joke played on him. He read it as a lack of respect and a put-down.

"You should have reminded me. I was in your office twice yesterday." Even though George knew he was wrong, he blamed Eddie.

"No problem," Eddie said, "we can still get it done." But George was angry.

George not only found it difficult to laugh at himself, he also rejected compliments.

"Great job last week," a colleague had said.

"I could have done it better," he immediately replied, "but I had so little lead time."

George had loaded himself up with such high expectations that he couldn't possibly fulfill them all. It's not that unexpected disappointments crop up every now and then, but that falling short of his goals is inevitable. Yet, every nonsuccess increases his hostility.

George copes with his "failures" by working harder. More than anything else he wants to feel busy. The results of his work no longer seems to matter so much. The ultimate importance for George is to be working. The means have become the end for him.

I can identify with George. I came to my first job as pastor of a small rural church with a tremendous need to be successful. I remember being called to the hospital late one night. I went, not so much to bring comfort to one who was dying, but so I could tell others the next day that I had been there.

"I'm really concerned about Chris," I would say, "I spent the whole night with him at the hospital." I wanted people to see that I was committed to my work. The inconvenience of staying up all night gave way to the impression that I was important.

If others failed to recognize my "dedication," I became angry. After all, I had paid the price. They owed it to me to be impressed. To make sure that they were, I announced that I worked harder and longer than any member of my church. I carried within me a vague resentment of anyone who failed to put me on a martyr's pedestal.

"They make me angry," I would say, avoiding the fact that I caused my own hostility. As long as I blamed someone else, I never had to come to terms with my own behavior.

George and I have many things in common. Like him, I feared other people. Somewhere I missed the message that I could be loved for just being me. I grew up thinking love was always dependent upon my deserving it. The problem came when I realized that I could never trust a "bought" love. Do they like me or only what I do? I kept asking, "Will they still love me if I do not perform for it?" I was caught in a trap. The more I wondered, the harder I worked, and the harder I worked, the more I wondered. It all seemed so unfair, leaving me with a helpless feeling expressed in a hidden hostility — just like George.

In a way, my fears were greater than George's. Not only did I mistrust others, I feared God. (George does too but he would never admit it.) I worked to earn God's love. I believed that God knew my unworthy motives, so I had to work even harder to qualify. I assumed that God was against me, that God related to me on a cause and effect basis and that my only hope was to *win* God over to my side.

Only after I had heard over and over again that God loves unconditionally did I begin to consider that possibility for me, too.

"There is nothing you can do to move God to love you," I heard Burney Overton say. (He directs the counseling service in our church and continually seeks ways to help depressed people trust in God's love for them.) "It's in God's heart to love; you never have to earn it."

For years, I had heard that God loved only the faithful and good. This salvation by works had been drilled into me for so long it was almost impossible to replace it with unconditional love. It's easier to believe God loves me when I deserve it than to trust God's love for me when I know I'm unworthy. That takes faith.

Until this day, I seek out the fellowship of a church that will reassure me of the unconditional love of God. I need to hear of God's grace again and again, but I am gradually beginning to trust it.

I met Robert Schuller one night on a late flight to Atlanta.

"What's your sermon about this Sunday?" he asked.

"Hope," I responded, flattered that one of the most popular preachers in America expressed interest in my sermon schedule.

"Wonderful!" he said, waving his arm in the air. "Do you know that Americans spend fifteen billion dollars a year fighting depression alone?" I listened as he affirmed my choice to preach about hope.

We talked for an hour. Then he asked if I knew a certain minister of TV fame.

"I know him."

"What do you think of him?"

"Don't like him," I responded, "but the aspirin producers love him."

"I don't follow you," Schuller said.

"All those depressed people are not outside the church. Many of them sit in our pews. They listen to us."

"Go on."

"Our friend preaches salvation by works. You are saved, according to him, by keeping the law and earning your way to the top. Yet none of us ever produce enough good works to feel secure."

"I'm sure that's right," he said.

"When you work as hard as you can and still fall short, you become depressed . . . and angry. It all seems stacked against you."

Later, as I remembered this conversation with the famous man of Garden Grove, I thought of George who felt so hopeless. He lives by the law which says only the best will make it. Yet no matter how hard he works, he never feels he has it made. He lives all his life by legalisms, and he is hostile.

The cost of legalism is always hostility—and hostility uses time badly. Changing our conception of how God loves us, from "earned" to "by grace," will make possible more and more *kairos* time—to share with others, even to spend on ourselves.

5   The Down Side of Uptime

"And our new vice-president is. . . ." The chairman of the board paused dramatically. "We are happy to name George McCullough our new vice-president."

Half of the board of directors and the entire front office clustered around to congratulate George.

For George, the announcement seemed like a dream come true. He had worked for this moment all his life. *The payoff, at last,* he thought: *a higher salary, a title, and an auspicious office.*

Five hours later George sat alone at his desk, staring into space. The biggest day of his life and he felt sad.

On special occasions George poured himself a drink or two, just to celebrate. That night, George surely had cause. He reached for the bottle in the lower left drawer.

Six drinks later, George felt as if the room were spinning. He staggered to the sofa. "Whoops," he said out loud. "Too much on an empty stomach." He fell asleep. The next thing George knew, he had vomited all over himself.

He felt better, at least for a moment. But he was a mess. What could he do? He took off his pants, cleaned them up as best he could, carried them down the hall, and laid them over an air vent to dry. Then he fell asleep again.

Three hours later George woke up confused. He walked

toward the corridor to retrieve his trousers. Just as soon as he pulled his office door shut behind him, he realized what he had done. There he stood outside the office in his shirt, tie, and jockey shorts with no key to get back in.

The security guard could come along any minute, but if George could get to his car, he'd have a chance to get home. He kept a spare key in a magnetic hide-a-box under the bumper.

Down the back steps he went, afraid of being spotted at any moment. He slipped out a back door and felt another wave of panic as it locked behind him. He made his way behind the bushes, sliding against the wall until he felt safe enough to run for the parking lot. It was cold and George moved as quickly as he could across the open spaces to his car. *Thank God,* he thought, *the key was still there.*

Twenty minutes later George banged on the door of his home. After several identification shouts, Doris let him in. She was shocked and he could think of no satisfactory explanation.

"Something terrible must have happened today," she said.

"I honestly don't know," he answered. "But something's not right in my life." Then he began to cry.

At that moment, 3:30 in the morning after his great promotion, George was closer to facing himself than he had ever been before. For the first time in his life he acknowledged a crack in his armor. Always before George talked about all that he had *accomplished.* Then suddenly, in a moment of panicked truth, he was forced to see what he had *become.*

"Am I an alcoholic?" he asked his wife.

"I don't know," Doris answered. "But whatever you are, I don't like it."

Again, George cried harder. He had finally achieved what he wanted—he was vice-president. Yet when he achieved it, it didn't feel like what he wanted anymore. Something essential was missing. He had made it but who, besides himself, really cared?

George's problem was deeper than his alcohol. Drinking

seldom interfered with his work. His sadness grew out of his lifestyle. The "shoulds," "oughts," and "musts" that dominated his life promised him great satisfaction when he "arrived." But they lied to him. The loneliness of almost total self-centeredness robbed him of satisfaction. George the image, was strangling George the man to death. No matter how many others were forced to *respect* him, Vice-President George still hungered to be *loved*. His superman ego finally submitted to his need to be one of a family.

"I'm struggling with post-achievement depression," he told his secretary a few days later. "Sort of like some women feel after having a baby."

"You should be on cloud nine," she said. "It's what you have always wanted."

"Yeah," George said. "I don't know what's wrong with me but something is."

Some would say that what George felt after his promotion was predictable. They suggest four reasons why George struggled with his new role of vice-president.

First, George struggled with the extra work.

George already carried about as heavy a load as he could shoulder. He had made it up the ladder by working longer and harder than anyone else. He had been Johnny-on-the-spot to volunteer for any special assignment. "No problem," he would say with a laugh, as he took on added responsibilities.

He frequently promised his family, "Just as soon as I get past this unusually busy time, I'll slow down." With this promotion, that would not be the case and on a subconscious level George knew it. He would be busier than ever.

As he thought of his new position, George groaned. He felt tired. "Bone tired," the old farmhands described it. George knew what they meant and he felt it. He was like two people fighting a civil war within. One was ambitious, the other very tired.

His superiors had placed great trust in him by this promotion. Now he would have to prove himself worthy of their confidence. But could he? George honestly didn't know.

Second, George struggled with guilt.

"It's the American way," he proclaimed. Every son is expected to do better than his father.

"Cream always rises to the top," he explained. All things considered, a man like George naturally surfaced and took his place of leadership.

"I deserve it," he told Doris.

But behind all his efforts to convince himself that he got the promotion because he was the best qualified, he felt inadequate. "If they really knew me," he said to himself, "I wouldn't be here." He knew some others who could do a better job but he seldom allowed himself to admit it.

George had "bought" his promotion. For twenty years he had watched the pecking order at staff meetings. He had made sure to agree with his immediate superiors, and never missed a chance to point out how someone else had failed. At times George even withheld information to swing things his way, but not too often. He was not a devious person at heart. Sometimes he climbed up on someone else's back. He had paid for his position, yet buried inside he fought to keep down a twinge of conscience.

On the night of his promotion George missed his father. He would have given anything if Dad could have been there with him. Dad would have been so proud.

Remembering Dad created conflict for George. If anybody had ever deserved a promotion, his dad had. Yet Dad was always passed over. "You let other people walk right over you," George remembered saying a few years ago. Now, suddenly, George identified himself with the "walkers." No telling how many dads he had stepped on, and he felt guilty.

Third, George struggled with self-doubt.

He was a sitting duck for that catastrophe known as the "Peter Principle." According to its author, "In a hierarchy every employee tends to rise to his level of incompetence."

When a man reaches fifty, he slows down, George thought.

Younger men not only have more energy, they often produce fresher ideas.

If I'm not careful, George thought, some thirty-five-year old kid could replace me. So he worked longer and harder than ever before. Could he keep up? Would he push himself beyond his ability? He didn't know.

Fourth, he struggled with the realization that this would be his last promotion. Time would run out before he could make president. He never expected to, but suddenly it seemed within his grasp. If only he had been made vice-president a few years ago, he would have had a chance. Now George knew he was too old. Time had run out.

Time, he thought. *It was always the timing.* All his life he seemed "off time," a little too late.

He remembered becoming a Boy Scout on his twelfth birthday. Sonny Collins, his best friend, had joined the troop four months earlier. All through their scouting careers, the two of them received similar recognition and had earned their ranks at about the same rate. Then the time came when they both knew it would be their last year. One of them would be named Senior Patrol Leader. George already knew Sonny would get it. Sonny got a four-month head start on George and everything George did was a little behind Sonny. As hard as he tried, George never could seem to make up those four months.

Now, half a century later, still trying to catch up, George would miss it because he was too old. In seven years, when the company president retired, George would be too old for the job. "I can't get the timing in life to work for me," George once said. "I often feel that I'm either too early or too late. It's not fair."

All four of these feelings: guilt, overload, doubt, and frustration whirled around inside George as he faced his promotion.

"Vice-president," they had said. Just what he had always wanted. But sometimes the scenery looks far better from the bottom of the hill than it proves to be up close. Oscar Wilde had this in mind when he said, "In this world there are two

52 The Gospel for the Clockaholic

tragedies. One is not getting what one wants, the other is getting it."[1]

"I finally got what I wanted," the little boy said, "but I don't want what I got." That was true for George, at least for a period of time. He felt depressed after his promotion. In spite of the big "step up the ladder," his life seemed to be sliding downhill.

When he said to his wife, "Something's wrong in my life," George wanted things to be different. He wanted out of the rat race. He was at a crossroad. For years he had felt some tugging inside but always covered it up by working harder. Then, suddenly, a hard-earned promotion failed to give him the rewards he expected. Now he could choose to change, he could ignore his inner voice and step up his pace. If he does, George is setting himself up for burnout.

Burnout has been described as "a state of fatigue or frustration brought about by devotion to a cause, way of life, or relationship that failed to produce the expected reward."[2] The term brings to mind a building which has been gutted by fire. All the insides are destroyed. All that remains intact is the exterior. It looks okay but it's only a burned-out shell.

"I'm tired of the rat race," George said. We can visualize an experimental rat running in a cage shaped like a wheel. He holds the illusion that he's really moving up hill. In reality, he's only spinning the wheel faster and faster.

I remember feeling like that rat. I pushed harder and harder just to stay in place. If someone had asked, "How are you?" the only honest answer I could give was, "I'm tired." I've lived my life on edge. Like George, I wanted out.

I looked to Scripture and found the words of Paul. "Do you not know that in a race all the runners compete, but only one receives the prize? So run that you may obtain it" (1

[1]Oscar Wilde as quoted in Herbert J. Freudenberger and Geraldine Richelson, *Burn Out: The Melancholia of High Achievement* (New York: Doubleday and Co., Inc., 1980), p. 54.
[2]Herbert J. Freudenberger, *Burn Out: The Melancholia of High Achievement* (New York: Doubleday & Co., Inc., 1980), p. 13.

Corinthians 9:24). I wanted to say, "Thanks a lot, Paul, just what I needed." I already knew I was in a race. Only it was a rat race, not a marathon.

Paul's prize seemed too vague for me. I wanted wealth, power, popularity, security, and love. If I couldn't have all of them, I would have settled for any one of them.

I had cheerleaders to spur me on.
— "Give it all you've got."
— "Put your shoulder to the wheel and your nose to the grindstone."
— "Think big, make every minute count, seize every opportunity," and above all, "believe in yourself."

So I did.

I would leap out of bed, jump into my clothes, dash to work, and plunge into my day's routine. Then I'd run out for lunch, spend the afternoon making calls, wind it all up by five and beat it for home. That was my rat race and I was very tired.

Julia Ward Howe once said, "I'm tired way down into the future."

I have felt that way and when I was that tired, I was not myself. I did and said things that I would never have thought of had I been more rested. Such "bone tiredness" acts on the body like a drug. It dulls the mind and deadens the senses. All tiredness is not the same.

Some tiredness is physical and can be overcome by sleep and rest.

I know a chaplain who used to say, "If you have a problem, take the weekend off. Sleep, eat, swim, and relax. On Monday, if you still have a problem, come and see me."

Some tiredness, however, comes from *frustration*. Life gets so routine, with few easy victories and even fewer permanent victories. Win today and we have to do it all over again tomorrow. Most tasks, even completed, have to be repeated.

Yet psychologists say we can stand almost anything as long as what we do has purpose. We may get tired *in* it but not tired *of* it.

For this reason, the cure for burnout is not just rest, but faith. As long as I can see my day as moving toward God's plan for my life, I feel replenished by a mystical energy.

Julie Ward Howe was tired. But she felt God stirring her on. She wrote a song that set a nation of men marching.

> He has sounded forth the trumpet
>   That shall never call retreat,
> He is sifting out the hearts of men
>   Before the judgment seat
> O be swift my soul to answer him.
>   *Be jubilant my feet,*
> My God is marching on.

In the same way, when my life seems no-win, and dead-end, when depression follows my victories, I seek for more reason for faith rather than more rest.

6   Clockaerobics

As George put on his coat, Doris looked up. She asked, "You're going out *again*?"

"Won't take long. Have to finish up."

She sighed, "This will make the twenty-second night in a row. So will you schedule me for one evening next week?"

"Twenty-second?" he said, ignoring the rest of her remarks. "Aw, c'mon. . . ."

Doris took her husband's hand and led him into the kitchen. A calendar, prominently displayed on the refrigerator door, showed a long series of red X's. He quickly counted. Tonight she would add number twenty-two.

"Honey, I'm sorry, but there's only one of me, you know!"

"I'd like to see a little of that one."

"All I get is pressure from home and criticism on the job," he exploded. "You'd think I was deliberately staying away."

"Aren't you?"

"Oh, come on, that's not fair. I just don't have enough time."

"You have twenty-four hours a day just like everybody else," she shot back. "It's a matter of priorities."

George left, angry and under greater pressure. But in his heart, he knew Doris had said it right: priorities. Although he wouldn't have admitted it, George knew he had never quite worked out the matter of priorities in his life. If he were not careful, he could spend *all* his time on the job. He felt more competent as a manager than he did as a husband or father. At any rate, he averaged working six days and five nights a week at the office. He worked as long and as hard as the best of them. If nothing else could be said about him at the end of his life, it may be said with accuracy, "At least he worked hard." He had no time-consuming hobbies and hardly ever took a day off. In fact, when he was not producing, he felt guilty and listless.

While some say, "When my ship comes in, I'm going to have enough money to do the things I want," George says, "When my ship comes in, all I want is enough time." He's never had enough time and he is tired.

A year ago George, complaining of being tired, had gone to see the doctor. "Even wake up tired," he told the doctor.

"George," the doctor said as he wrote out an unusual prescription, "take this and you will be okay."

It read:

Once a day for a week, drive to the center of Greenwood Cemetery. Look around. Take your time and notice the tombstones. Then say aloud, "Most of these folks were convinced that the world just couldn't get along without 'em." So slow down! You don't have to sell the entire world, not all by yourself.

George didn't follow his prescription and he's still tired.

He's not alone in this. Our whole society runs revved up. One businessman said, "I live at such a pace, if I miss the first section of a revolving door, it throws me off schedule for the rest of the day." We laugh at him, but we also groan a little, for he describes a bit of many of us. We often think the only way to succeed is to rush.

An old man carefully drove along the expressway at forty miles per hour. Cars zoomed by, drivers shook their fists at him as they risked a chance to pass. He was a driving hazard.

Finally, a patrolman pulled him over. "Old man," he asked, "do you know why I stopped you?"

"Sure," said the old man as cars sped by at seventy miles per hour, "I was the only one you could catch!"

George is afraid that if he slows down like that old man, he'll get caught.

He's also afraid if he slows down, that the world will run off and leave him. The idea that he may already have passed over more than he will ever catch never enters his mind. He uses long weekends and daylight savings time to squeeze in more work. Some call it the "BMB" syndrome—"Behold Me Busy." It's as though he owes it to God to be tired.

It's foolish to think God could find joy in his exhaustion. When George is tired, he doesn't think clearly or relate well to God, to other people, or especially to his family. When it comes to his work, *God doesn't call for George to be exhausted but rather to be responsible.* The long hours he puts in are not as much a sign of his great commitment to God as of his irresponsible use of time.

The relationship of quantity to quality in his work is little more than coincidence. In one sense George is a drug addict. He depends upon his own adrenaline to keep him going. He tells himself that he works best under pressure. But that's not true. He may work harder when he's pushing toward a deadline but that doesn't mean that he works better. He probably doesn't work as well as he would have if he had managed his time better, or more accurately, if he had managed *himself better in the time he had.*

Unlike pounds or talents, God gave to each of us an equal amount of time. It can't be stockpiled. We are forced to spend it at a fixed rate of sixty seconds per minute. We are responsible to God for our use of it. We never "make" or "save" time. We simply manage ourselves in the time we have.

The problem is to keep the *chronos* time from swallowing up the *kairos.* We often let the schedule ruin the trip. Concern for time prohibits us from enjoying the things we have scheduled to do.

I have known George for a long time. He made mistakes in managing his time which showed not only poor stewardship but left him physically, mentally, and spiritually spent. I have made some observations that could put him more in charge of his life.

George never planned. Every manager knows that "if you fail to plan, then you plan to fail." Yet most mornings George arrived in the office and jumped in on the first thing that caught his attention. He then switched to something else that needed to be done, often before he had finished what he started first. All day long he leaped from one little chore to another until time ran out. Then he would say something about how time had flown and what a busy person he was!

Of course George kept appointments, usually five to ten minutes late. It seems he spent half his traveling time rushing somewhere to be late. It was hard for him to learn but he had to admit that even when he planned a time to leave, he seldom left on time. He programmed himself to be late.

I have learned from George and today I'm doing better.

1. *I make an effort to leave early for an appointment.*

If I get there ahead of schedule, it gives me time to meet a new friend or experience the scenery. I never used to notice the architecture and landscaping of a public building. I was always in too big a hurry to see them. Now I carry something to read in case I have to wait, or I will look at the pictures on the wall, browse through books, or look out the window. Leaving early also relieves the panic of being caught in a traffic jam.

2. *I keep a legal pad on which I write out a daily schedule.*

I make it into a desk calendar using a page for each day, a new pad for each month. I write in things I need to do on future days such as prepare for a committee meeting, pick up shoes at the shop, or write a letter to Mr. Brown about so and so. Some things I schedule months ahead.

Each morning I check my list for the day and add to it current things carried in my mind. I write them down, no matter how impossible they might be to forget. This simple procedure eases the continual rush-hour pace in which I am prone to live.

Another mistake I used to make was in trying to carry my things-to-do list in my head. Invariably I remembered some important things too late. Now I write them down. With a list visibly before me, it's easy to put things in some order of importance.

3. *I concentrate on the things that really count.*

I used to tackle the easiest chores first, setting no priority on the more essential jobs. Now, I prioritize. If some of the nonessentials are left undone, it's okay. I've still had a productive day.

I even school myself to do the most dreaded task first. Whether it's making a phone call or working on some project I'd rather not do, I get it out of the way. That makes it easier going the rest of the day. I take the time to organize. Otherwise I postpone those unpleasant chores and live all day with them hanging over my head.

4. *I keep an orderly place to work.*

"A clean desk is a sign of a sick mind," George once jokingly said. He bragged about having a pile of work on his desktop for all to see. But a messy desk clutters. Some of the busiest executives I know keep everything out of sight except the one project on which they are currently working. I strive for that goal. I'm not trying to become an order-nut. I am working for efficiency, not neatness. A cluttered desk causes confusion and wastes precious time.

5. *I answer or discard all correspondence as it's received.*

Immediate responses keep me from having to reread it. If I need more information before a letter can be answered, I begin to research it now or schedule in my legal pad calendar when I will deal with it.

6. *I never carry an appointment calendar with me when I leave the office.*

When I'm asked to make a time commitment, I say, "Of course, but I'll have to check my calendar and let you know."This gives me time for second thoughts. I can always call the next day and beg off. "Sorry, but I have a conflict." The conflict may be that I need to stay home and rest. Also, keeping only one calendar avoids the embarrassing realization that I have scheduled two events for the same night.

7. *I have learned to leave space between appointments.*

A little slack time enables me to handle unexpected problems or take advantage of sudden opportunities. On the other hand, when I schedule appointments back to back with no break, I carry tension from one to the next. By the end of the day I am irritable and less effective.

I need interruptions. Most time management leaders list interruptions as a chief culprit but I usually enjoy them. Visitors and phone calls often let the only sunlight of the day into my office. To have a friend drop in and tell me a joke or share with me something of his day can often make the rest of the day's work worthwhile.

8. *I control my appetite.*

I'm learning, but I still make mistakes that have nothing to do with the calendar. I often eat too much for lunch. Then, for an hour or two, I'm dying to go home and sleep. I stick it out at the office but I'm sluggish. I do better if I have a light lunch. My waist does too, but that's another chapter.

9. *The most lasting mistake I make and the one most difficult for me to handle is feeling guilty about the things I don't get done.*

Every night when I come home, I carry a burden for those I did not see and the things I did not do. If guilt were a positive influence and motivated me to do better, it might be worth the destructive agony I carry inside. But guilt never helps. It only blocks. Perfectionism grows out of my insecurity, not my faith. It's the result of my fear that God won't accept me unless I earn it.

The good news of Jesus Christ is that we are valuable to

God because God loves us, not because we perform. God does not load us down. God calls us to responsibility, not to guilt. God sets us free.

George and I both seek to manage our time, but for different reasons.

He wants to do more things in less time. On the other hand, I want more time in which to do less.

7 Breaking the Clockaholic Habit

"I'd change," George said, "if I just knew why I drive myself so hard."

"No, you wouldn't," his friend Bill responded.

"What?"

"Wouldn't change," Bill said again.

"If I knew why. . . ."

"Wouldn't make any difference," Bill interrupted. "You won't change until you *choose* to change. Understanding *why* won't have anything to do with it."

"You sound pretty sure of yourself," George said, feeling a bit threatened.

"Yeah. I quit smoking."

"Good."

"Not because I analyzed why I smoked. No, I found a reason to quit."

"Like what?"

"Like when they cut out one of my brother's lungs trying to keep him from dying of cancer. It was then I decided to give up smoking. Haven't had a cigarette in four years."

George was about to speak when Bill continued, "People usually change when they are more afraid to remain as they are than to become something else."

Again George wanted to defend his idea that he could change

if he knew why he did the things he did. He was convinced
that something in his childhood caused his clockaholic patterns. But anything he could think to say sounded even to him
like an effort to escape the real issue. At last he found his
voice. "I was born in a hurry," he said, half laughing.

"No, you weren't," Bill said sharply. "You choose to live
in a hurry.'

For days, George couldn't get Bill's insights out of his
mind. He had never had anyone speak in such a candid way
with him. George really had chosen the rushed lifestyle and
he knew it. No one is born with bad habits, he thought. Habits
are the result of the deliberate things we choose to do.

Like the rest of us, George is a creature of habit. He gets
up each morning at the same time, combs his hair in the same
style, and drives the car the same way, all from habit.

Most of his habits are good. He couldn't live without them.
He would have a wreck within a block if he had to think about
how far to turn the wheel, how much pressure to put on the
brakes, and how many miles per hour the car moved at every
point along the way. He can drive now only because he learned
certain habits.

In the same way, George performs thousands of tasks each
day. He ties his shoes, drives himself to work, and types notes
without thought because he has committed these motions to
body memory. The first time he tied his shoes, he concentrated
on every move. He awkwardly moved each finger until the
knot was tied. Then he practiced each move until now he gets
dressed, listens to the news, and plans his day all at the same
time, and hardly remembers putting on his shoes.

Whether good or bad, habits have a way of getting hold of
us. They start with a single decision.

No one ever sets out to be an alcoholic. That destiny starts
with one drink, then two, until drinking becomes the most
compulsive force in life.

In the same way, George, at one point in his life, made a
decision to try to pack more into a period of time than he

could get done. That decision made it easier for him to set the same pattern again. By the third time, he didn't have to make a decision, the pattern was set.

Someone said, "We do something the first time because we want to, then we do it because we did it that way before. Finally, we do it because we cannot help it. The habit is formed." As in the old saying, "Sow an act and reap a habit; sow a habit and reap a character; sow a character and reap a destiny."

If we *form* habits by what we choose, we can *change* them the same way, one choice at a time.

George can change his unhealthy habits, not by seeking to understand why, but by choosing to change. Even for George, the clockaholic, Type A superman egoist, who is determined to accomplish more than anyone else in less time, there is a way out. But it won't be easy. To break the clockaholic habit, George must *change the clockaholic, not the clock.*

1. The first and most difficult step for George to take is to *admit he has a problem.*

He cannot continue his time-pressured pace forever without burning out. But he has an option. He can admit that he needs to change.

This will probably be the most difficult step he will take in breaking the clockaholic habit. George has a lifetime pattern of blaming everyone else for "causing" his uneasy feelings. It will not be easy for him to admit now that he is his own problem. Like the old saying, "I have met the enemy, and he is me," George must face the enemy he carries around inside.

2. He must not only admit he has a problem, *he must tell someone.* Expressing it out loud draws attention to it and it can no longer be hidden.

"I've got a problem," he said out loud to his wife, "and I'm going to do better," That single announcement made him obligated to himself and to Doris. The decision to change, if George keeps it to himself, won't do one thing for him. He must name his problem to another human being. An idea or impulse becomes real to us the moment we give it a name. When George confessed "something's not right," only then did he realize it enough to do something about it.

3. George *needs a partner.*

This step grows out of the previous one. George must find a special someone to whom he can say, "I've got a problem. If you struggle with time pressure as I do, maybe we can help each other."

Anyone who has ever walked the railroad track knows how easy it is to fall off. Especially when you first start, a puff of wind or an unexpected sound will cause you to slip. Get a partner, reach across to hold hands with someone else and the two of you can walk on the rails indefinitely.

The same is true in breaking a habit. Each partner can help steady the other.

God seems to have blessed us with a sixth sense. In addition to the physical five, God gives us one to tell us with whom we can share our inner being. But this sixth sense is not infallible. If George exposes his concern to someone who fails to understand or who has no desire to overcome the same addiction, then George will feel betrayed. He must then risk finding another. But something inside will direct him to the right partner.

George needs someone who will encourage him to put his personhood ahead of his production. Together they can set goals and support each other in having more free time. If a trusting relationship begins on the level of their measurable conduct, it can lead them into deeper things, like asking pertinent questions as "Why?" or "What am I trying to prove by all my busyness?" More important, partners may help each other to see the more relaxed, enjoyable persons they are each becoming.

4. George has to *take action.*

I remember a teacher once asking, "If three frogs sat on a log, and one decided to jump, how many frogs would be left on the log?"

"Two," Johnny answered.

"Wrong," said the teacher. "There would still be three." There's a difference between deciding to jump and jumping. Deciding to do something about his problem is the first commendable thing but taking one small step makes the difference.

Dozens of books tell how to change a lifestyle, to slow down and have more time for living. (See the Suggestions for Further Reading at the back of the book.) George would do well to read any of them. They share good, practical suggestions on how to change. The problem with most clockaholics is not a lack of program but that they take on *too much* at one time. Changing habits is like crossing a stream on stepping stones. We can step on only one stone at a time. The time-saving and attitude-changing suggestions found in this book alone would overwhelm us.

George would do well to pick *one step* and take it. Then the second.

For instance, George sees Eddie begin each morning by arriving five minutes early. Eddie sits at his desk and seemingly does nothing. He gives his mind freedom to contemplate the day. If George would simply give himself this one break, it might gradually change his entire life.

Habits never stand alone. Good ones or bad ones always gather others of like nature to support them. If George started his day claiming a few private moments, it would be only a matter of days before he could find more time for himself. Soon he might even think of himself as worthy of his own care. Then George himself would begin to change.

Whatever the first step, if George will force himself to honor it for just three weeks, it will become a new habit. It may seem awkward the first day or two. But whether George decides to meditate a few minutes each morning, take time to speak to others in the office, or to arrive five minutes early for appointments, if he will do it for twenty-one days, the chances are that George will have replaced a bad habit with a good one.

Experts say it takes three weeks to turn a deliberate action into a habit. Repeat an action twenty-one times and the subconscious begins to take over.

5. George needs to *do something just for fun.*

"Go to the ball game?" his son Phillip asked. "You mean this afternoon? Just you and me?"

George actually set aside Friday afternoon to take his son to a baseball game. He never remembered doing anything like this before. It was easy to rearrange his schedule to include an afternoon for recreation but not so easy to get emotionally free to do it. Even as they drove to the stadium, George tuned out Phillip's excitement in order to think about the things he "should" be doing at work.

As they parked the car, George wondered, *What if someone sees me?* He was entitled to a day off, but he felt as though he were "playing hooky." At least ten times he checked his watch, hoping they would start the game soon. Maybe it was going to be okay, but he couldn't have been more uncomfortable if he had been planning to rob a bank.

The next day he shared his experience with Bill. "I guess I enjoyed being with Phillip but it wasn't much fun for me. I felt I was cheating on everybody back at work. A lot of people were there, though. Wonder how they get time off?"

George struggled not so much with his schedule as with his guilt. He couldn't relax without feeling guilty. At least he could claim the ball game was for his son. He would have done just that, too, if anyone had seen him, "Phillip just *had* to come. You know how that is," he would have said. No matter what they might have answered, George would have heard them as saying, "Ah ha, slipping around on the company, are you? How do you explain this one?"

"Maybe a ball game was too much for you," Bill said. "Why don't you start with a crossword puzzle? Just for the fun of it."

"You've got to be kidding," George answered.

"Nope, dead serious . . . or even better, read a novel."

Haven't done that in years, George thought. *It might be fun to waste a little time . . . for me.*

6. George needs to *see God's work in his life.*

The best way I know to break the clockaholic habit and avoid burnout is to admit it, tell someone, take one corrective step, find a partner, do something just for yourself, and most important, to see God's plan at work in your life.

Believing in God results in two influences on my understanding of time.

First, faith in God gives meaning to my time.

Faith is not a "constant" with me. By that, I mean I don't always believe. I get busy doing so many things that I can go hours without giving a serious thought to God. Some days I even say my prayers by rote. But every now and then I stumble on a *kairos* moment. This awareness of God in my life may come during an act of worship or while looking at a beautiful scene. Suddenly I feel that God is alive, that God knows my name and that I'm OK and life is OK, because of God.

I don't keep those moments of awareness. They fade as quickly as they come. My mind shifts to dozens of other things, but that split second of God-consciousness *adds meaning to the rest of my life.* It makes sense out of my whole week.

If there is no God to share my life, if my time here does not lead to a continued life beyond, then what's the use? No matter what I do, each day I get older and weaker, and too soon I die. For what? That's the unique thing about human life. It's never content just to live. It must have something to live for. It must have meaning.

Second, faith in God allows me to leave my future to God. I don't have to do it all now. Even if I fail, *my* failures are not God's failures. As pious as it sounds, God can use even my mistakes. I can leave some things undone. I'll always feel that there is more that I *could* do than I *can* do.

Perhaps this is one of the messages to us from the creation story in Genesis. "But of the tree of the knowledge of good and evil you shall not eat" (Genesis 2:17). From the very beginning, God limited what humans could do. God does not expect me to do everything. God has others who can do things I can't and many of them do it better. God holds me responsible only for those things I am able to do.

The most important decision George can make in easing his clockaholic habits is to believe that God works through his life. Without such a faith he will try to cram a week into every day and shoulder the burden of making his own life sufficient to meet all of his needs. He will fail. Time will run out and George will die. He will see himself in partnership with God or he will burn himself out seeking to produce his own security.

It's a matter of choice. If George will live as though God is at work in his life whether he "feels" God or not, God will soon become a habit to him.

"Is God a habit?" George asked.

"Seeing God in my life is a habit," I answered. "The best I know."

8   Guiltless Kairos

"Another cup of coffee?" Doris asked.

"I wish I could," George replied, "I just don't have time." One minute and four seconds later he rushed out the door. At least he had plenty of gas in the car.

Later that morning a colleague asked, "How about lunch?"

"Sorry," George said. "Can't take the time until I get this project finished."

After supper, Andy approached. "Can you come to my game tonight, Dad?"

"Oh, son, I wish I could but I've got to finish this income tax. I had so many interruptions on this that I've hardly gotten started."

"I understand," Andy said.

"I really want to see you play, son. It's just that I don't have time."

George had enough time. At least, he had more time than he was willing to admit. When he said, "I haven't time," he meant, "I don't have time *for you*. I'd rather do something else." He then lists all his activities to prove that he really couldn't do what he had already chosen not to do.

It's easier to say, "I don't have time" than to be straightforward and admit that "my priorities leave you out." But that's precisely what George was doing. He knew it and he felt guilty.

Time priority enters into the success or failure of almost everybody I have known. Time is one of the most common denominators known. Every person on earth has twenty-four hours a day, with no variation since Adam. The president of the United States and the most worthless bum on the street share the same 168 hours a week. The difference lies in how we choose to use it.

"I knew exactly what I wanted in life," Richard said. "I wanted to be a millionaire by the time I was forty. I made it. I own a business, travel, and can buy almost anything I want."

"That's impressive," I said.

"But I'm the most miserable man in the world," he added. "I hardly know my children and my wife wants a divorce. I don't know what success means any more."

Richard exemplifies many others who have plenty to live on but little to live for. A year later all that had changed. Richard chose some new life goals. He decided that relationships were more important to him than amassing great wealth.

From time to time, Richard will slice out a day or two. He and his wife will get a live-in baby-sitter and go to a motel for the night. They enjoy doing things together: eat a good meal, go window shopping, spend some time doing "other things," eat blueberry pancakes for breakfast, and come home. They often have a fuss. Yet they talk and share more in this short twenty-four hours together than they used to do in twenty-four weeks. At home the only time they had to talk was late at night after the children had gone to bed. By then they were tired. Things didn't seem the same when they were tired.

To patch up their marriage, they scheduled one night a week just to talk. No matter how late Richard came home, his wife would wait up and they talked. They belonged to a small sharing group—of two members.

Richard also plans prime time with each of his children. It's impossible to be available to all three of them at once;

usually the older ones feel left out because the young ones demand the most attention. So Richard schedules a night out with Dawny. They go to a ball game or do whatever Dawny wants to do. It's just the two of them and they talk without interruption. The next free night will be Dad's night with Betsy for shopping or eating out. Bill is the youngest. Going with him to the mall or watching planes take off at the nearby airport not only gives them time together but allows a more relaxed time back home. Bill loves to go anywhere, just so it's with Dad. Then after these special times with each of his children, Richard starts over.

This personal time with Dad also helps the children understand when Richard says he needs some time to be alone with Mother, his wife.

Richard has found other ways to strengthen his family ties. On the Christmas tree, Richard hangs IOU's: "This card entitles Martha to a night of bowling with Dad," or "This card is good for one fishing trip."

As soon as Richard gets a calendar for a new year, he blocks out special days. He marks off birthdays, anniversaries, holidays, and times off. Once he was asked to speak at a banquet. "Sorry," he said, "but that's my daughter's birthday."

"Surely you could celebrate with her at another time."

"Don't think so," Richard replied. "You can find others to speak to your group. But I'm the only father Betsy has."

Richard has decided that it's imperative for a busy person to make time for his family. He now has life goals that are clear to him and worthy of his efforts. Even at work, Richard's "nows" have more meaning. His priorities allow for *kairos* time in his schedule.

Even Jesus set priorities on his use of time. He couldn't do every good work or heal every sick person. He chose the best use of his time and moved on. He actually turned away from people in trouble and left work undone to withdraw and be by himself. He left Capernaum to go to Jerusalem. In a sense, even Jesus said, I don't have time for you, I choose to do other things.

Jesus' example comforts me. If Jesus, the one person who lived a life of total obedience to God, could walk away from work, it gives me freedom to choose. At times I must leave the office no matter how many phone calls need to be made. Unlike Jesus, I don't have God-wisdom. Sometimes my choices are unclear.

I have little difficulty in setting the first, second, or even third priority in my use of time, but the fourth through twentieth get muddled. Some needs are clear: if my friend stumbles, I will stop and help him; on most days the decision to go to work is automatic; on most Sundays I want to be in church. I have chosen to be a caring, productive, and religious person. But what about the choice between visiting a friend in the hospital or staying home to rest because I'm tired?

It's not hard to distinguish between the good and the bad. We all do that easily. But sometimes it's difficult to distinguish between the good and the essential. If it's show up at work or lose my job, the choice seems clear. On the other hand, what if the choice is between going to Jim's ball game or working on income tax?

In a case where two goods vie for the same time, I consider two factors in making my choices.

First, *I consider the context*. It makes a difference whether it's April or Jim's birthday. It matters how long it's been since Jim and Dad had private time together and how close they feel to one another. It also matters whether Dad can find another time to do his tax work. No action stands alone. It has a history. Those things that have gone before and the circumstances surrounding it determine the meaning of any event, spoken or done. That's what I mean by context. Most of us consider context without a second thought. We feel its influence and make decisions accordingly. We automatically drive more slowly when it rains, sleep more when we're sick, and run faster when we're late. Context determines most of our action. Yet much of our context we neither control, nor would we choose. The context in which I live today is determined mostly by the choices I made yesterday.

Some people argue that there is only context and no such thing as the present. "Now," they say, "is that fraction of time that cannot be divided into a smaller part. It's infinitesimal and instantly turns a future which is not yet into a past which is no longer." They say we can measure the past and the future, but what we measure is the absence of the present which has no existence.

Others argue exactly the opposite. "We live in an eternal now. No matter how great the memory of the past or anticipation of the future, we always live in the 'right now.'"

These views of time claim to contradict each other. Yet I agree with both of them. We live in the now, which is never free from the influence of the past and which, in turn, determines the future. Another way to say the same thing, "If I didn't plan tomorrow yesterday, then I am a prisoner of today." Many people have no idea of where they are going, for they lack goals. They simply spend each moment reacting to the events of their past. In choosing the best use of my "now," I consider its context.

Second, *I consider my life goals* in setting time priorities.

This reminds me of an old story: The professor asked a young student, "William, why do you want to attend college?"

"So I can graduate and attend law school." William answered.

"Then what?" the professor asked.

"Then I will join a successful law firm and earn a good living."

"Then what?" the professor asked.

"Then someday I would like to be elected a judge."

"Then what?" the professor asked.

"Then I will retire."

"Then what?" the professor asked.

"Then, well, then," William said, "I guess I don't know. I haven't thought that far."

"Go home," the professor said, "and start all over. You have begun at the wrong end."

Many of us, in time, go through motions and accomplish enormous feats without any clear ideas as to why. I believe that nothing we do now has much meaning unless it moves us toward a predetermined life goal that is clear and worthy.

Time management writers stress the importance to set aside a special time to review. Go to a special place every few months, they say, and ask yourself if you have accomplished all you set out to do. I like this suggestion. Only I want to go to a special place and *review my life to evaluate what I have become, not what I have produced.* More important to me than *doing anything* is *becoming* what God wants me to be.

I am learning from Jack. Almost a month ago Jack closed his office for two days. "I need some time to get my bearings." Jack has a very successful medical practice and he seemed to know exactly what he was doing with his life.

"I spent two days all by myself," he said. "I asked myself four questions: Where am I? How did I get here? Where do I want to go with my life? and How do I get there?"

"And?" I asked.

"I'm going to rethink some of my priorities," he said.

I have never taken two days off for self-assessment but I am committed to five minutes a day. I ask myself if I am moving in the direction I want to go. If so, I need special time for myself, with special others in my life and with God. To protect these quality times, I'm willing to say, "Sorry, I don't have time," to many other demands.

Because he felt his life was significant, Jesus paced himself. He planned his ministry and took the time he needed for rest.

I believe my life is important, too, and I have no right to waste it. There's no need for me to rush. My life span is only a segment of all eternity. I am moving toward that time when *kairos* and *chronos* are one and I will certainly keep that appointment on time. But while I am here, I seek without guilt to manage my *chronos* time that my *kairos* days may be full.

9   Living from Then
Till Now

"**S**orry," the receptionist said. "Mr. Newey's not in."

"But this is the third time and he promised. . . ."

"I'm sorry, but. . . ."

"When do you expect him?"

"Tomorrow."

Bang! George slammed down the phone. What good would it do to shout at the receptionist?

George sat at his desk with his heart racing and his hands trembling as he rehearsed out loud the speech he was determined to deliver to Mr. Newey.

"In the first place, you promised to deliver that table two weeks ago. Then yesterday I stayed home all day, waiting. And I still don't have my table. What kind of people am I doing business with anyhow?"

Being late was one thing, George thought, but to make an appointment and not keep it . . . I certainly don't have time for that.

For most of the afternoon, George drifted back into his plans to criticize Mr. Newey. Tomorrow would be slow in coming and George hated to wait. He was angry *now*.

Next morning George intended to call Mr. Newey "first thing." But when he arrived at the office, other matters had to be dealt with.

"Morning, George," Eddie said, "Beautiful day, isn't it?"

"Yeah," George muttered, walking through the office.

"Morning, George," Betty said, smiling. "Thought you did a great job at the meeting last week."

"Thanks."

"Oh, George, can you give me a few minutes?" Eddie said, following George to his desk. "I don't know how to respond to this budget request."

For fifteen minutes George dealt with the ordinary affairs of beginning a new working day. Finally, at 8:55, he got around to calling Mr. Newey. By this time, though, George was no longer angry. Yet the problem remained. The table had not yet been delivered. The memory of yesterday was still fresh, but the emotions had subsided. In a pleasant voice George said to Mr. Newey, "I had to step out yesterday for about thirty minutes. Hope I didn't miss your truck."

What a difference time can make. We often remember the good experiences of bygone days while forgetting the bad. "I remember the thrill of my son's birth," a young mother said, "but I have long forgotten the pain of it." She speaks for most of us. The anxiety of adolescent years fades away, as does the grief of the death of a childhood friend. We remember the good times of college days but have forgotten the long nights of grinding study. Most of the past pains of life lose their potency in time.

Time often heals.

But not always. Time worked in George's favor. Marvin, though, is another story.

"I'm sorry," the doctor said, "medical science has no cure."

Marvin struggled to maintain his composure. "Give it to me straight, Doctor. How much time do I have?"

"No one knows."

"A year?"

"Possibly."

"But not likely?" Marvin asked.

"We just don't know," the doctor said.

Inside Marvin knew, but he didn't know if he would be able to face the ordeal of dying.

"A year's a long time," Marvin's wife said. "They'll find a cure—you'll see."

"Time doesn't cure cancer," Marvin said.

For six months Marvin grieved over his upcoming death. "Not enough time," he said. "I want to see my children grow up, to be with people, and to do my job. It's not fair."

All grief comes back to the same thing. We run out of time. We have too short a time with those we love. The experience of life ends too soon and God seems to have turned away from us.

"I don't know what to believe about God anymore."

"Please, Marvin," Marie said, "You mustn't give up. Trust God. Tomorrow will be better."

Marie was wrong. The next day brought more pain and less hope. Marvin felt that God had betrayed him. "I'm running out of time and where is God now that I really need him?"

"You must be patient. God works on his own time schedule. You can't rush him," she said, not really knowing what else to say.

Marvin waited . . . and prayed . . . and grew more discouraged. "God, you promised that those who wait upon the Lord shall renew their strength, they shall mount up with wings like eagles." The Psalms say, "God is our refuge and strength, a very present help in trouble," God, where is your help?

Marvin expected God to keep these promises and everyday he grew more frustrated.

Although our situations differ, I can understand Marvin. Twenty years ago our second son was born. "Blind," the doctor told me. "He also has club feet, cleft palate, and we suspect that he may be spastic and retarded."

I asked the same questions expressed by Marvin. "Why did

God let this happen to me?'' I had always been a believer and had pledged my life to serve him.

"You're unfair," I said to God. "You made a mistake." Give God enough time, I thought, and God will correct it. "Everything will be all right," I announced. Yet, twenty years later, it's still not all right. Gene is still retarded. But I'm no longer angry with God. Time heals.

Not only do I understand Marvin, I think I understand myself. Most of my frustration grew out of wrong expectations of how God's promises would be fulfilled. My problem was not in my experiences but rather in my expectations. It's the same old story. *Illusion* gave birth to *disillusion*. God had not deserted me, but what I thought *ought* to have happened shaped my interpretation of what *did* happen.

God fulfills promises to help us in three ways.[1]

First, sometimes, *God helps us by intervention.*

He becomes "our refuge and strength, a very present help in trouble," by *rescue*. God comes into our life and changes things.

At the pool of Bethesda, Jesus healed the man who had been paralyzed thirty-eight years. Jesus changed his circumstances.

Sometimes God intervenes and alters the situation. To me, God did that with Gene's eyes.

I pleaded with God. "Oh, please," I sobbed, "don't let my son be blind." I could already foresee all the frustrations and limitations on his life. "Please, God, don't let it be this way." One night I stayed for hours on my knees on the garage floor. I cried and bargained.

The next day brought a change in Gene's circumstances. "We have run some more tests," the doctor said, "and now we think he may not be totally blind. At least we feel certain that he can see images and motion." From that day on, Gene's sight steadily improved. He wore glasses at eight months that

[1] I am indebted to John Claypool for this concept.

made him look like the cartoon character Mr. McGoo, but he was not blind.

I can't explain what happened, but to me it was a miracle. My faith allows me to say, God intervenes.

Intervention is the first kind of help I want—and often demand. Let me get in trouble and I cry out for God to change my circumstances. Sometimes God does.

I make a mistake and set myself up for disillusionment when I think this is the only way God helps.

Second, sometimes, instead of rescuing me, *God helps by collaboration.* He chooses to help by inspiring me *to discover my own resources.* God says, "Do it yourself."

Nehemiah cried over the condition of his kinsmen who were back in Jerusalem. He pleaded day and night for God to remove their troubles. Then God spoke to his heart and Nehemiah himself went home to rebuild the city. Even though his workers had to carry a tool in one hand and a weapon in the other, they built the wall. "For the people had a mind to work" (Nehemiah 4:6).

Often God does not change the circumstances for us. God calls us to use our own tools and weapons.

I thought that if God could remove Gene's blindness, God could solve all the rest of Gene's problems. I prayed, and nothing happened. I prayed some more. "Lord, if you will just fix him, I will give you praise." I had never really expected miracles from God, but I had never felt the need of one so bad. I watched "The 700 Club" and "Oral Roberts" trying to learn the right language or formula to claim a miracle, but nothing worked.

I remember feeling very alone. Nobody could get to me. Nobody could feel the emptiness that had suddenly clouded my life. Rather than miracles, every day it seemed the news got worse.

"We recommend surgery for his palate," one doctor said. "Take him to Atlanta."

"A cast for his legs," said another, "take him to Memphis."

"He'll need special treatment for his eyes. There's a good doctor in Tupelo."

"Six months in the Diagnostic Center in Jackson will tell us what we're up against, but it will be expensive."

Everything was expensive. I borrowed from insurance, parents, and friends, but we made it.

Today Gene has lived half his life in institutions. He has experienced more surgery and pain than all the rest of our family added up together. He has cost us thousands of dollars every year for special shoes, braces, therapy, and transportation.

Yet, today, he has surpassed every expectation I ever dreamed possible for him.

Looking back, I was never alone. I had friends, family, and a host of medical ingenuity to support me. Their efforts became God's collaboration. Rather than intervening by removing the problems, God forced me to seek the resources around me. God worked through the skills and love of others to help in my deepest needs. Just as God said to Nehemiah, you do it and I will be with you.

Third, sometimes *God gives us the power to endure.* He allows us the strength to stay with something we cannot change.

Paul prayed three times for God to remove the thorn in his flesh. "But he said to me, 'My grace is sufficient to you, for my power is made perfect in weakness'" (2 Corinthians 12:9).

Gene is still retarded. Many more than "three times" I begged God to make it not so. But Gene will be retarded all his life.

I can remember days when I thought his affliction was more than I could take. Gene absorbed my emotions, energy, and money. There was a time when I felt that I could never love him. He was a burden to me so I begged God to change Gene.

God gave me only the strength to endure. I couldn't change the circumstances, so *the circumstances have changed me.*

Now I enjoy Gene, although he is still a burden and always will be. He is a funny kid. I laugh at him and with him everytime we are together. Life shortchanged him in many ways but God blessed him with his own brand of humor. Most of the time he is a pure delight.

I love him. Maybe it's the simple way in which Gene accepts his dependence, but most people seem to love him. Gene is an open book, with no games or power struggles. He sees nothing but beauty in every other human being. I have learned from him not to take myself too seriously. I am also reminded when I am with Gene how *I* must look to God: retarded and totally dependent. I can no more earn God's love by performance than Gene can earn mine. Yet I love Gene in spite of his inadequacies. I believe God loves me in the same way.

I feel better about Gene now. As I look back over the years, I am aware that God has enabled me to endure. But Marvin's life offers no promise.

What does Marvin do when life seems to stop? When the present circumstances feel too unbearable to survive. "I remember the good days of the past," said Marvin, "and maybe sometime in the future things will be better, but what about now? What do I do now?

Often, the hardest part of living in time is *waiting*.

I feel as if I'm always waiting for something to happen. I wait for some glimmer of daybreak, for someone to come, or to get well. I've spent much of my life in line waiting for an appointment, or my turn in a doctor's office. But Marvin has only the interim, somewhere between what used to be and the not yet. How can he survive in the interim? I think the Bible offers some help.

A half a millennium before Christ, a man named Jeremiah lived in the interim. He wrote to the Jews who were in exile in Babylon. They were a long way from home. Their hearts screamed with the memory of those whom they loved and of things that used to be. Their hearts were either behind or ahead of them. How could they survive?

When we are caught in the interim, when we're bound and broken down, Jeremiah says, "Build houses and live in them; plant gardens and eat their produce" (Jeremiah 29:5).

Jeremiah is saying when we are caught in an unpleasant now and have to wait, then do the ordinary, next thing: "Build houses and plant gardens."

Jeremiah also says when you're caught in the meantime, "Take wives and have sons and daughters" (Jeremiah 29:6).

He is saying that if we have little else, we have family and friends. When we can't pay our own way, when we have no strength, when we can't even beg, we still have one another.

When we are forced to wait, seek life where we are. The most enlightening thing Jeremiah said to those caught in foreign lands is that their peace depended upon the peace of their captors. "But seek the welfare of the city where I have sent you into exile, and pray to the Lord on its behalf, for in its welfare you will find our welfare" (Jeremiah 29:7). When captured, put down roots there. That's the only place we have to live. We can save the flags of yesterday and paint dreams of tomorrow, but we live where we are now.

The amazing thing is that when Jeremiah's captives sought to live where they were, they served and sought God there. When they did the next thing, maintained their fellowship and dug in their roots, *they found that they had been found by God. God was there, even in Babylon, all the time.*

So we, too, will continue to struggle, to listen, and to love. We'll maintain the fellowship. We'll hold, and touch, and kiss. We can be the church to one another, especially when we hurt. We can put down our roots and seek the welfare of where we are now, and in doing so, we can find God.

The interim brings nothing to an end. It's only one step in a long progression.

Someone said, "that which appears to be an *end* of time is simply the *edge* of time, in which we may discover that we have been found."

Earlier I said that time often heals. In reality, *time* never heals. It's God working in time who actually heals. Some things, like resentment, mental illness, or broken relationships may deteriorate in time. Days and years can become a merry-go-round in which life gets faster and faster until we're dizzy. But time may heal.

That which makes the difference is not time itself but *the direction in which we move in time.*

Many people live from yesterday, which they think of as sure, to an unpredictable tomorrow. With money in the bank and insurance policies they seek to avoid the anxiety of the unknown future.

Those who believe in God live in the opposite direction. We live from the end to now. *A Christian lives life backwards.* Death, which is the ultimate anxiety for an unbeliever, becomes the beginning of new life for those who trust the promises of God. The future is no longer uncertain and therefore holds no threat. Tomorrow is sure. Marvin may still have a savings account and insurance, but his basic direction in life can be from a joyful end to an unpleasant now.

"Just live one day at a time" is meaningless if life is based only on the past. But *if tomorrow is sure, the journey through time is healing.*

If this life is all we have, then time has no meaning. Each day we hurt seems to last forever. But if the promises of God can be trusted, and "a thousand years in thy sight are but as yesterday when it is past" (Psalm 90:4), then why fret over a day so short?

I live with the promise of the backward life for George, Marvin, and Gene. I believe the day is coming when George will no longer be anxious, Marvin will no longer be sick, and Gene will no longer be retarded. *Ultimately, God will intervene.*

That's why Jesus said, "Do not be anxious about tomorrow."

10   The Inner Self Has the Last Word

"**F**ive days?" George asked. "I don't have time to be laid up for five days."

Dr. Read knew George well, and this response to hospital confinement was no surprise. Yet, he had no choice. The kidney stone had to be removed.

"Five days is a minimum. Why don't you give yourself this chance, George, for your health?"

"Nothing was wrong with my health. At least, not until this stone. . . ."

"But what causes kidney stones?" Dr. Read asked.

"I don't know. You're the doctor."

"I don't know either, but I have an idea."

"Okay," George said. "Let me hear it."

"Stress."

"Stress causes kidney stones?"

"Stress, depression, and guilt, I'm convinced, are all related, not only to kidney stones, but to cancer, heart disease, stroke, and a hundred other physical disorders that plague us."

"So, you're saying . . . ."

"I'm saying that I can remove your kidney stone and you can be out of here in five days — —"

"But?"

"But, I can't make you well. Only you can do that."

"How?"

"By a change in your lifestyle."

"You think it will come back, I'll get another kidney stone?"

"George," Dr. Read asked, ignoring his question, "What do you do just to take care of yourself?"

"I don't know," George said, "I guess if I'm honest, mostly, I work."

"Then let's at least give you a five-day rest."

Two days later George checked into the hospital with surgery scheduled for the following morning. Three days later George felt like himself again, anxious. He lay in bed feeling guilty for not being at work. So much to do and every day George fell further behind.

Yet Dr. Read's question nagged him. "What do you do to take care of yourself?" George couldn't think of one thing. That trip last year to visit Paul was supposed to have been restful. Yet George couldn't enjoy it for fear of losing out in his drive for success.

On the fifth day he pleaded with Dr. Read. "If I don't get out of here, doctor, I'm going to lose my mind."

"Take it easy, George, or you may never get out of here."

"But you promised five days."

"Provided you don't blow a gasket."

Ten minutes later George lay thinking, not because he wanted to but what else could he do? He would rather be *doing anything* no matter what, or going somewhere, no matter where.

George behaves like the businessman I heard about who ran to catch a bus. He barrelled down the entranceway steps, touching every third one. He looked like the typical New York businessman in grey flannel suit, umbrella in one hand and briefcase in the other. If he missed this bus, he would be fifteen minutes late and in trouble all day.

Running for the corner, he jumped over several street kids playing marbles on the sidewalk. "Hey," he cried, "hold the door." Then, a little old lady stepped off the bus right in his path. He grabbed her by the shoulders, spun her around, kicked over a wire litter basket, hesitated, dismissed the thought óf picking it up, and jumped on the bus.

Just as the door closed behind him, he brushed himself off, gained his composure and said, "Excuse me, driver, but is this bus number forty-one?"

"What?"

"Where is this bus going?"

George, like that man, rushes to get somewhere, ahead of time if possible, but he's seldom sure of just where.

He struggled in the hospital because he was forced to stop and think about where he is going. How much better if he could stop from time to time to reassess his life. George has been running from himself so long, he is afraid of his inner self. Unless forced to, he won't acknowledge that other self.

Human beings have the ability to be two persons. George can see himself from outside and analyze his own personality. He can argue or even fight with himself.

One reason he stays busy is because he doesn't like the other George, the insider. He tries to lose this inner self in the hectic pace of external activities. He drives himself with work, occupies himself with responsibilities, and drugs himself with alcohol. Given half a chance, George could evade learning the truth about his insecurity and success syndrome.

Then came the hospital. No work to do. He lay quietly and alone. The inner self caught up with him and said, "Hey, you can never totally get rid of me. No matter how hard you run, you can't escape my inner tugging."

Then Dr. Read's words, "I can't make you well unless you do something about your lifestyle." Those words echoed over and over again in the heart of George's inner self.

"Where are you really going, George?" he asked himself.

He didn't know. He had never learned to get in touch with his inner self.

I've asked myself that same question. Like George, I can

keep so busy that doubts about me get blurred into an uneasy
anxiety. In recent years I've been learning a process to get in
touch with my inner self.

First, I find a place where I can retreat.

Time managers quickly advise executives to find a time
when they can reflect on the previous year. "Look critically
at what you have accomplished," they say. "Be honest and
admit all that you have left undone." Unfortunately, they often
urge a rescheduling to accomplish even more in the future.

My inner self tugs at me with another kind of question. Not
"What have you *done* in the previous year?" but rather *"What
have you become?"*

I deal with this kind of self-interrogation better in a retreat
setting. When I try to crowd inner-self questions into the
context of routine activities, I seldom get below the surface.
My inner voice comes in a whisper and gets drowned out. It
gets confused with other sounds. If I am to hear, or more
accurately, to feel the cry of my soul, I need a *place apart*
from the racetrack of everyday activities.

My place is home, not the house where I live now, but the
homeplace where I grew up. At least once a year I visit my
parents and childhood neighbors who for half a century have
lived next door. When I visit home, it's like stepping back
into the days of my roots.

Invariably I find myself bragging to the neighbors about my
accomplishments. I want them all to think I left home and
"made it." I remember all the stupid stunts I pulled as a child
and I want desperately for my old neighbors to conclude that
I am now in control of all my life. Yet, mixed with all my
successful adult image is an inner child asking, "What have
you really become?"

Home is the place of my dreams. I used to sit on the side
steps and talk to myself about the kind of person I wanted to
be "when I grew up." I could see myself as a loving husband
and a dedicated father. My friends would always love me, and
the next crop of five-year-olds who came along would admire

the person I had become. Naturally, I would forever be honest, kind, smart, and generous.

Now, forty-five years later, I still sit on those steps surrounded by scenery almost unchanged and ask myself if I have become the man I dreamed I'd be.

In all honesty, I have accomplished more and achieved recognition beyond anything I ever dreamed. But I'm not the person I set out to be. I have a long way to go. At home I renew my dreams. I have no choice. I can have peace in my life only when I have peace with my inner self.

Second, I honor inner-self priorities.

I am learning to be more aware of my self-needs.

For instance, I have learned to say "no" to other people, even to neighbors, children, bosses and ministers. "I'm sorry but I can't spend that time with you," feels okay for me now, at least most of the time.

Other people, often without realizing it, develop an expectation of me. They communicate certain values and activities that I must honor or I disappoint them.

"You will come by and let us show you the way we have decorated the new den, won't you?"

"No, but thank you."

"But," they say, "it would mean so much to us."

"I'm sure it's beautiful, but let me see it another time."

"It would only take a minute."

By this time in the conversation, I am at a crossroads. I can give in and spend a segment of my little free time meeting someone else's needs, or I can choose to do something that I want to do, even need to do, just for me.

There was a time when I spent *most* of my efforts filling the expectations of others. I soon realized that twenty friends with a 5 percent claim on my time would wipe me out altogether. I am learning to say "no," without guilt.

Anytime I sacrifice what I expect of myself for what someone else expects of me, I'm paying too high a price.

Saying no was hard for me in the beginning. I feared others

wouldn't like me unless I did what they expected of me. I couldn't tolerate the feeling that just one person thought I was not the best. So, I often said, "yes" when I really wanted to say "no."

There are two problems with "bought appreciation" logic.

In the first place, people seldom like me because of what I do or fail to do in order to impress them. Real friendship gets sabotaged by efforts to buy it. Purchased appreciation carries the seeds of its own destruction. I never know if they care for me or only for the things I do.

Also, if I think others like me because I never say no, I don't like myself. I feel as if I have sold myself to anyone willing to pay the price of liking me. I feel cheap.

I am learning to be more selfish about my life and claim time for me when I need it, without guilt.

I recognize three inner-self priorities for my time.

One, my inner self demands time for *meditation*.

I can get so involved in catching the bus that I fail to notice where it's taking me.

Some of my most valuable time is spent in meditation. This may not be the way for anyone else, but here's how I do it.

I find a quiet room where I know I won't be interrupted. I soften the the lights and sit in a comfortable chair. I become aware of my breathing, taking deep breaths, and trying to allow myself to relax. I start with the top of my head and mentally relax every muscle of my body all the way down to my toes. After relaxing the body, I try to put my mind at ease. I picture peaceful scenes and let my mind wander from one pleasant thought to another. I call to mind a favorite biblical text.

This process of relaxing the body takes only about five minutes.

During meditation, when the body is still, sometimes the mind becomes more active. I become aware of memories and feelings which usually get surpressed by activity. Rather than try to block out my thoughts, I honor this as a time to re-evaluate. I think about God's claim on my life.

In meditation I seek not so much to confess my sins, but to *confess myself*. Sins make me think of certain acts. When I confess myself, I admit my strengths as well as my failures. I talk to God about my total being.

This is not a time in which I heap guilt upon myself but rather a time to redirect my life. My inner self demands that I take time out of my busy schedule to reassess the purpose of all my busyness. Meditation is my number one inner-self priority.

Two, I seek *introspection*.

I ask myself some hard inner-self questions such as:

- How is life with me? What kind of person am I? What is my life all about?
- Who am I? Where did I get this self-image: from my parents, from God, or from where?
- What do I think of my body, the medium through which I experience the world? Am I weak or strong? What do I do to take care of my body? In what ways do I abuse it?
- What do I think of when I think of myself? Am I an introvert or extrovert? Am I a feeling person or a rational person? Am I happy or sad? What gifts do I have? Do I accept myself or do I condemn myself? What changes would I like to make?
- What are my dreams? How am I going about fulfilling my dreams?
- What are my primary values? What is important to me? What do I spend my time doing? What do I think of most? What angers me? What delights me? What are my values doing for me?
- What are my commitments? What am I giving my life to? Who are the significant people in my life? What do I give them? Can I name anything for which I am willing to die? Can I name anything for which I am willing to live?

- How important is God to me? How real is God to me? How real am I to God? How important is Christ to me? How important is my church to me?
- What do I think God is calling me to do with my life now?

I ask these questions one at a time in an effort to catch the right bus.

Three, my inner self demands time for *play.*

Play is not the same thing as recreation. I feel sorry for the man who owns a battery-operated golf cart. He's got to play golf every week whether he wants to or not, just to keep his battery recharged.

Play happens when we lose track of time. I remember as a child playing catch in the front yard. Suddenly, Mother called us in for supper. I had no idea it was that late. Play transcends the boundaries. When children jump and climb trees, they transcend the limitations of gravity for a moment. In the same way, when I play, I transcend the limitations of time.

It's not as easy for me as an adult to find ways to lose myself in time and play. Flying did that for me. I remember renting a small, two-seater, canvass-covered airplane with the wheel on the tail. I crawled in, and the plane took off and climbed up as high as its eighty-five horsepower engine would take me. Then I throttled back and glided all over the county. I made a game out of trying to land without adding power. I liked being up in the air, alone, with the window open. I sang and talked to myself. I even called out to the high-flying birds as I sailed by. On those days, from the time I buckled in until I landed, I never thought of time, job, world affairs, or obligations. I simply had fun.

Today I have no activity that quite gets me away from it all like those days of fun flying, but I am looking. Taking pictures helps a little. Occasionally I take a day off with Tommy, my college-age son, to drive through the countryside with our cameras.

"Look, Dad, there's a contest winner," as he points to an old barn.

"For sure!" I say.

We ride along the country roads and talk photography all day until it's too dark for pictures. As I come home late for dinner, my inner-self says to me, "It's *kairos* time. You need to do this kind of thing more often."

"For sure," I answer.

Four, my inner self demands that I *take care of my body*. That means:

Exercises - I do sit-ups. It's quick and requires no special equipment, training, or clothes. Calisthenics not only develops muscle tone and helps me feel better physically, it relieves tension, makes me more alert and confident.

Yet calisthenics alone fails to strengthen the cardiovascular system. Aerobic exercise increases the efficiency of the lungs, heart, veins, and arteries to deliver oxygen to the cells. Jogging (without driving to excel), swimming, cycling, or any steady repetitive exercise opens the blood vessels and strengthens the heart.

But I don't overdo it. I've seen the faces of joggers who looked as if they suffered agony. I believe calisthenics and aerobics should be enjoyed. I listen to my body—when it hurts, I ease off. More important than how strenuously I work is how frequently I exercise.

No matter what program my exercise takes, my energy level slows down if I skip it altogether.

Nourishment - The times that I have forced myself on a strict diet, I have gotten into trouble. I cut down to 1,200 calories a day one time. Not only did I feel tired after a week, I suffered six hours of amnesia. So I don't crash diet. I cut back, don't stuff myself, and watch *what* I eat rather than *how much* I eat.

I also consider where I eat. I seek a cheerful time and place for meals. Rushing through lunch when I am angry or distressed causes me indigestion. Stress sabotages the whole digestive system. I prefer to eat with friends in a pleasant atmosphere.

Rest - I try to nap every afternoon but I usually make it only about four times a week. Research shows that those who break the work day with a twenty-minute nap perform better than those who take coffee breaks. The older I get, the less nighttime sleep I seem to need but the more I benefit from short breaks in the day to read, talk with a friend, or daydream. At any rate, I am learning to listen to my inner self when it demands proper exercise, nourishment, and rest.

My inner self keeps requesting more time for me.

Like George, I can refuse to give in. "All those things sound good," he said, "I just don't have time."

George spent two weeks in the hospital, this time. If he doesn't learn to heed his inner self, it could be six weeks next time.

One way or another, the inner self has the last word.

11   Time for Others, Health for Me

"**E**ddie's son has had an accident," Betty said.

"Is it serious . . . ? How did . . . ?"

"They've taken him to DeKalb General," she said, "Eddie got the call when he came in. Rushed right out of here . . . seemed pretty upset."

George paused. "As soon as you hear anything, let me know."

Betty turned to leave. Then stopped. "I can cancel your appointment this morning . . . if you want to see him."

"Hadn't thought of. . . ."

"You and Eddie have been friends a long time."

"Yeah. You think I should? Maybe you're right. I'll go."

"I hope you find it's not too serious," she said.

"In fact, I need to see Mr. Beasley. I'll stop by his office on the way back. But I'll be here in time to keep my luncheon appointment."

What a way to start the day, George thought, as he pulled out into the street. *I'll have to put a rush on to see Beasley. I'd better go there first.*

Already, George knew what was going to happen this morning even though he would not openly admit it to himself. He would see Beasley. It would take longer than he allowed. Heavy traffic would not leave time to visit the hospital before

his lunch appointment. George would not get to see Eddie.
That's exactly what happened.

"How's Eddie?" Betty asked as he entered the office at
11:47.

"Didn't see him." George responded. "Didn't have time,
I'll go this afternoon." But he knew differently.

George had made a choice. He could have spent his time
either doing business or visiting with a friend. George chose
what was most comfortable for him. He was sure of himself
in business, but not so certain in friendship. Later that night
when George went to bed, he would think of Eddie and feel
a tinge of guilt. He would also be pleased about the business
with Mr. Beasley. Most of all he would feel *lonely*.

Loneliness dominates his life. In spite of his accomplishments, George has no close friend. He can take care of business
with ease but he rarely shares his feelings.

"What's bothering you, George?" his wife, Doris, asked.
"You're so withdrawn tonight."

"I don't know."

"Something happen at the office?"

"No. Anyway, I don't want to talk about it, Doris, not
now."

"If not now, George, when? We never talk, you know."

"I never have time just to talk."

"And you never have time just for me," she said. "I don't
even know you anymore."

"Sure you do," George said with an edge on his voice,
"I'm the one who pays the bills."

Doris didn't say any more. *George was just being George,*
she thought.

All his life, George had searched for meaning. He looked
for it in those places they told him it could be found. When
he started elementary school, they told him, "If you get an
education and work hard, then you'll be successful. Accomplishment is the only way to the good life."

George became a succeeder. As vice-president of a major

corporation he could afford to "pay more bills" than he ever dreamed possible when growing up. But George was not happy. He was lonely.

Like George, I was a good succeeder. I served as pastor of a thousand-member church, earned three degrees, published books, and received more speaking invitations than I could accept. All the cultural identification tags labeled me "successful." Yet I, too, felt lonely.

I gradually reexamined the tracks on which I was running. All my hard work failed to fulfill my inner needs. "Surely, there must be more to life than this," I said.

Then one day I discovered something strange to me. *Jesus seemed to call people out of work and into relationship.*

"Come, Levi," Jesus said, "follow me."

I can hear Levi, "Wait a minute, Lord, I've got books and papers spread all over this table. Who's going to tally up all these accounts and balance my books? Look at all I have to do."

If I had been Jesus, I would have said, "Oh, yes, I understand. You have all that work to accomplish. Why don't I come back on Friday around five o'clock? If you've got it all done, then you come follow me."

To Peter and his brother, Jesus said, "Follow me and I will make you fishers of men."

I can hear Peter say, "But Lord, if I don't catch fish who's going to feed the children? I must work."

If I were Jesus, I would have said, "Oh, yes. Work is most important."

Not Jesus. He told them to leave their nets. To be with him was more important.

I don't believe Jesus would ever have been hired to work for George's company. I can just imagine Jesus filling out an employment application.

"Okay, Jesus. Just fill in your name there and on the second blank you put your occupation."

Jesus says, "Occupation—oh—well, I used to be a carpenter."

"We're not interested in what you used to do. What is your occupation now?"

"Well," Jesus says, "I walk around."

"You . . . your occupation is to walk around?"

"Well, yes. I talk to people and I listen to them."

"Oh," George would say, but Jesus wouldn't get a job.

Jesus seemed to think relationships were more important than jobs.

Once on his way to Jerusalem, he stopped by the home of his friend Lazarus. Mary came and sat at his feet, talking and listening to him.

Martha, working in the kitchen, called out to Jesus, "I don't understand you and Mary just sitting there talking with each other while I slave away over this stove. I'm working. Why don't you tell Mary to get in here and help me with my work?"

Jesus responded, "Mary has chosen the good portion" (Luke 10:42).

They both searched for meaning in their lives. Martha assumed it could be found in *production*. When Jesus came, the only way she knew to serve him was to feed him.

But Jesus wasn't hungry. He was on his way to Jerusalem to face death and he wanted to talk. Mary sat at his feet and listened. I am trying to learn from Mary. She had found a better way.

I don't think I'm going to find meaning in my life by becoming a company executive. Meaning is not found so much in my work as in my *relationships*. I do not imply that work is bad. It's necessary and good. But work is *limited*.

How badly I need to remember that. When I get depressed and feel empty inside, I immediately ask, "What must I *do*?" I foolishly think that if only I could do more work, things would change for me.

I could ask a better question. Not what can I do, but rather *with whom can I be?* The time I spend with others is the most meaningful time of my life. But I have to make it happen. I can't count on chance or luck to place me with friends as often as I need them. I set goals for spending time with others.

First, I cultivate those who make me feel good.

For years I sought to be with those who did not like me. For instance, I spent unbelievable amounts of emotional energy trying to win Lillian's appreciation. I never did know why she was so critical of me but she seldom missed an opportunity to put me down. So I went to see her.

"Lillian, I'm uncomfortable with our relationship. I wish we could talk out whatever separates us and be friends."

"Why?" she said.

"Because I want. . . ."

"I don't need your friendship."

For thirty minutes I tried to absorb her jabs and break through the separating wall between us, but I failed. I left more discouraged than when I came. For the next two months I thought of Lillian every day. Finally I went to see her again. The same thing happened. She rejected every effort for reconciliation. All in all, I went to see her five times. Any time I saw her, in a store or at church, I went over to be in her company. I would go out of my way to speak to her every chance I got. All to no avail.

It took me a year, but I finally learned my lesson. Lillian doesn't like me. Now I go out of my way to avoid her. Why should I continue to subject myself to her abuse? I still don't know how I made her so angry, but I can accept the fact that I'm not her cup of tea and let it go at that.

I no longer feel that I must be liked by everybody. Thank God, I'm *somebody's* cup of tea. I have friends whose eyes light up when I walk in. They appreciate me and when I'm in their presence, I feel ten feet tall. I've learned to cultivate these kinds of friends, for they are very important people to me. I make special efforts to be with them.

I'm like my car. Regularly I have to drive into a service station or my car will run out of gas. In the same way I periodically stop by and visit a friend who "fills me up" with affirmation. If I don't, I run out of emotional gas.

I am attracted to people whom I consider as bright or brighter than I am. I can build relationships with dull people, but given the choice, I gravitate to those people who are sharp, seek to be outgoing, and who share at least one common interest with me on which to build a relationship.

John lives six miles down the road from me. We are both in ministry, have experienced similar problems, and enjoy a rewarding sense of compatibility.

I call John and ask: "Hey, Buddy. I need to have lunch with you. How about it?" Lunch with John means so much to me that I'll set aside work to be with him and cultivate his friendship.

Second, I take time to be friendly.

I start small. I show concern in the tone of my voice when I say "hello." I take time to look others in the eye when I greet them. I make a special effort to befriend those doing the less desirable jobs in life. Everyone recognizes the doctors and beauty queens. Few of us have time for the servants and elderly.

Keith Miller tells of his experience while buying gasoline one day. The station attendant spoke to him. "Good morning, Mr. Miller. It's nice to see you."

Suddenly it dawned on Miller that he had been buying gasoline from this man for eight years and didn't even know the man's name. Miller saw the name "Charlie" written on the attendant's uniform and decided to learn something about him.

"Charlie," he asked, "you got a family?"

Charlie was shocked when he realized that Mr. Miller actually wanted him to answer.

"Yes, sir, I got a family. In fact, we got five children."

"Tell me about them," Miller said.

Charlie went down the list giving a brief account of four sons and a daughter.

A week later Miller read in the newspaper that one of Charlie's sons scored three touchdowns for the local high school team. That afternoon, Miller congratulated Charlie. He also drove out with the cleanest windshield in town.

I believe such "thirty-second islands of caring" reward us with more meaning in life than lording it over others can ever offer.

I keep a little alphabetical address book in my billfold to help me remember people. When I meet someone for the first time, I write his or her name under the letter *where* I met that person. For instance, I wrote Bert under "C" for I met Bert working at the cleaners. The next time I stopped in to pick up clothes, I looked up "cleaners" before going in. Walking through the door, I called Bert by his name. It takes a little effort but it turns an everyday chore into a meeting of friends. (As I wrote this, Bert called and invited me to go fishing with him.)

I have learned that any effort to establish friendship rewards my life with love and purpose.

Sometimes I think our American culture, with all its emphasis on production, robs us of the time necessary to establish relationships as other cultures do.

By contrast, last year I visited Ghana, a poverty-stricken country in West Africa. Four of us traveled through dozens of poor villages. In each one we were treated the same.

We would ask for a meeting with the chief. An hour later he received us. He sat on one side of the room flanked by a dozen elders. We sat across from them and waited. Then he invited me to come stand before him.

"*Akwaaba*" (You are welcome), he said.

"*Medaase*" (Thank you), I responded.

"*Wohotazen*" (How are you?).

"*Moho-ye*" (I am well).

"*Aya*" (Good).

After that five-statement exchange, I would step over to the elder sitting on the chief's right. We shook hands and started the exchange all over. After I had been welcomed by each elder in turn, the next member of our group went through the same procedure. Then after all four of us had been welcomed by each of them, they came one at a time to our side of the room to receive our greeting. The process for four of us, and twelve of them, took over an hour.

On the tenth day of our journey we spent the night with our guide. As we entered his "home," even though we had already lived together for more than a week, he greeted us with the same lengthy ceremony of welcome. I learned that the *time invested to establish relationship was very important* to Ghanaians. In spite of their poverty, they have much to teach me about being friendly.

Third, I am learning to take time to listen.

I am convinced that the greatest need in the world today is not for new machines on the moon, or for a bigger bomb, but for a chance to be heard. We all need someone to hear our story.

Luke tells us of the woman who touched Jesus. She had suffered with an issue of blood for twelve years. The law of Leviticus condemned anyone with an issue of blood as unclean. She was barred from every social circle, even from worship. She felt like a nobody on the inside. Yet she believed that if she could touch the hem of Jesus' garment, she would be healed. Reaching through the crowd, she touched his robe, instantly became whole, and she knew it.

Mark says Jesus turned and said, "Who touched me?"

Then in the next verse, "And [she] told him the whole truth" (Mark 5:33). Jesus ministered to her by listening to her story. He moved through his life listening to people tell their stories.

As a pastor I have learned that most people don't need me to solve their problems. They desperately need me or someone *simply to listen to them and try to understand.*

Listening is hard for me. It takes a special effort. Often, when someone starts telling me something, I hear about 10 percent and jump gears. I shift off and start working out in my mind how I am going to respond. I try to impress the person with my great intelligence so I work out my answer . . . often before I have even heard what's being said. Sometimes I give beautiful answers to questions never asked. My best relationships grow out of my listening more than my talking. Listening helps me overcome my preoccupation with myself. Others get tired of my steady drumbeat of asserting my own importance. The best way for me to come alive and to escape my own internal loneliness is to listen to another tell his or her story.

Fourth, I find healing in confession.

I work hard to appear adequate. Like many, I hope that people think what they hear and see of me is all there is. I want them to believe I have no real problems just because I pretend that I have none. Sometimes I pay almost any price to keep from recognizing myself as I really am. No one can see the gaps and negatives I carry around inside, because I wear a mask. It feels safe that way. Also I pick up some form of diversion. I watch ball games, join groups, or play board games. I wear such a mask until there are times when I hardly know my bogus self from the real me.

"Who are you," a friend asked, "when you are not a professional?"

"I am always a professional," I confessed.

Yet I know I am not who I say I am. My past is just not as I choose to remember it. I have been programmed more to conceal than to reveal.

In all honesty, there is an animal in me. Several. The fox in me thinks I can exist only by my cleverness. The hog in me eats too much and basks in the sun. The cat in me is lazy and thinks the world owes me a keeping. But there is also a dove in me that hungers for peace. You see, I am a whole zoo.

Yet I am also a man, which means I am the keeper of the zoo. My inside name is Legion.

Remember that story. There came a demon-possessed man to Jesus out of the graveyard. The tombs were home for him, for he believed demons lived in those desolate, lonely places like that ravine.

Sometimes this poor man spoke in the singular, as if he were in control of himself. Sometimes he spoke of himself in the plural, as if many over whom he had no control dwelled within him and spoke through him.

He came to Jesus. "What have you to do with me, Jesus, Son of the Most High God?" (Mark 5:7). But he also "ran and worshiped him" (Mark 5:6).

Jesus heard his feelings, not his words, and asked, "What is your name?"

A name, in those days, meant more than it does now. A name described and controlled a man. If you knew his name, you knew every secret about him. Only a fool would tell his name unless it was to someone in whom he had great trust.

"My name," he said, "My name is Legion, for we are many" (Mark 5:9). He was confessing that there was a madness within. "I'm not what I appeared to be, I am many. I don't control myself. I hurt and run from myself."

He confessed to Jesus who he really was.

I believe healing was in his confession.

I respect the Roman Catholics because of the value they place in confession. Yet I'm not sure real confession ever comes when scheduled. Healing confession grows out of *relationships*. I need a caring friend with whom I can confess my real self. I need someone to whom I can say, "My name is Legion. I don't know how I got this way, I don't like it, but this is who I am."

I need to hear, "I understand, Tom, and I love you."

I find healing in that kind of confession. I have learned to take time to *communicate* with a special friend.

Communicate means more than conversation. I can converse all day long about money, schedule, and politics and never communicate. I communicate when I tell you of my inner feelings, my hopes and fears, and seek your understanding. I have found healing in that kind of communication.

All in all, the time I spend with others, whether for affirmation or confession, results in *health for me*.

I can't make it through life without spending time with others.

This concept reminds me of a lesson I learned in my Boy Scout days. It takes three logs to keep a fire going. It would seem that one log with enough flame and ventilation would do it, but not so. For some reason, it takes three logs together to keep any of them from going out.

In the same way I need some special friends to keep my life from going out.

I read that geese fly 73 percent farther in V formation than any one goose could alone. The vortex from the wings of the lead goose lifts those behind him.

I think that's true also of me. I can go further with the help of others. I take time to be with friends.

12   God Time

"Tom . . . I need you." Doris spoke calmly on the phone, "Now!"

"What's wrong?"

"It's George. He's had a heart attack," she screamed the last two words and sobbed.

Twenty minutes later I entered the quiet waiting room. Doris was crying. Several other people stood around but no one spoke. I wondered if George had died.

Doris looked up, saw me, and came over. I put my arms around her and for a moment we simply stood together. "We tried to tell him, didn't we?" she said. "But he wouldn't listen."

"Doris, any news?"

"They haven't told me anything yet."

I took her arm. "Why don't we step out for a minute and say a prayer?" Then all we could do was wait.

Later Dr. Read came in with good news. He expected George to live, but his condition would remain serious for days.

A week dragged on before George was strong enough to talk to me. His first words were, "Tom, I'm scared and I don't know God."

George's words shocked me. Throughout his life, he had

attended church occasionally and had even been elected to serve a term as an officer. Yet George seldom expressed serious thoughts about God. "I don't know why they'd make me an elder," he had said, "I don't have a lot of time for it."

Now, suddenly, George had time for God. "I thought I was going to die."

"That frightened you?" I asked.

"Yes . . . it still does. Tom, I'm terrified."

I touched his arm and waited. Then I said, "Seems to me that God is giving you another chance, George. God is as close to you now as ever.

"But I don't know God," George insisted.

Many of us, like George, place God on the back burner until we face a crisis. Then we suddenly become serious.

"Do you know," George said, "that on the average we sleep eight hours a day, work eight, eat for an hour and a half, and spend an hour getting dressed? Put it all together and that leaves us with more than five hours a day with nothing to do. That's thirty-five hours a week in which we can choose our activity. Yet I always said that I didn't have time for a closer life with God. I seldom prayed and never studied the Bible."

I was amazed at the speech George delivered. He had obviously been thinking about it for some time. "Sounds typical," I said.

"Why is it that we leave God out of our lives until something forces us to turn to God?"

"I don't know, but we do."

"Like there are no atheists in foxholes, huh?"

"Nor in funeral homes or ICU wards." I added.

George always believed in God, so he said. Yet, like many of us, only a time of trouble caused him seriously to acknowledge God.

Day by day George had chosen to live a double life. He patronized God, gave God a tip, and pictured God in regions far removed from the space and time of daily life. Yet he never completely cut God off. George wanted God "for emergency use only."

Every now and then God would tug at George's heart. Like when he drove late at night and listened to music, or when Andy asked why God made the snow, or when he sobered up after being promoted to vice-president. At *kairos* times like those, George felt a hunger for God in the everyday events of life. Most of the time, George, like one hundred twenty million other Americans who never darken the door of a church, avoided the "God question" as much as he could. Supermarkets, superhighways, and superficial living kept him sufficiently preoccupied. He seldom recognized his dual life, with an inner dimension.

When I look at George, I am reminded of the great biblical leader Moses, who, in a way, also lived a double life.

Outwardly, Moses was the Prince of Egypt, heir to the throne of Pharaoh. Inwardly he was a Hebrew and heir to the covenant of God. In his confusion Moses committed murder, ran away, and spent years roaming the desert in search of himself. Then one day, high on a mountain and alone, he stumbled across a burning bush, and there he heard the voice of God. "Put off your shoes from your feet, for the place on which you are standing is holy ground" (Exodus 3:5).

Never again did a double life plague Moses. He knew God's purpose for him.

In the hospital George cried out for a burning bush. He wanted a clear voice to declare that the ground on which he stood was holy, or at least acceptable, so he, too, could ask, "Who are you, God?"

George's heart attack had become his burning bush. During his lifetime, George had walked past numerous burning bushes and had never taken time to "turn aside and see."

The universe itself glows with burning bushes. God could have made the world bland and colorless but instead, he filled it with music, sunsets, oceans, and springtimes. Remember the saying,

> "Some call it autumn,
> Others call it God."

In a million ways God invites us to recognize deity in the everyday. We so often miss hearing God because God seems to call in a *whisper*. God only gives a hint of his presence.

Significantly Isaiah said, "The Lord God has opened my ear. . . . I gave my back to the smiters, and my cheeks to those who pulled out the beard; I hid not my face from shame and spitting" (Isaiah 50:5-6). Isaiah puts *listening to God* in the same category as being beaten, being spit on, and having his beard pulled. It's not easy to listen.

When God speaks we can never be sure it's God. Other people standing nearby may not hear or see anything. When Paul heard the call of God, those with him only heard thunder and saw a great light. The voice of God can usually be confused with other things. When God called Samuel, it sounded like the voice of Eli.

I want to cry, "Oh, come on, God, make it obvious." Am I to stake my life on something so fragile as the splendor of the sunrise, or a child's smile, or the faith of a dying friend? Or as with George, on the fear of losing control of his future?

"It's so uncertain," George said that day in the hospital, "If God would only light up a burning bush for us."

"Maybe he has," I said.

"Where?"

"Maybe this whole business of *Sunday* is a burning bush," I added. Sunday calls us to turn aside and *remember* God.

Nothing is too trivial or important that we can't forget it. We forget obligations, promises, names, enemies, and even loved ones. We can even forget God. Moses did. That's why God gave him a burning bush. And that's why God has given us the sabbath. Alongside the commandments regulating murder, adultery, and idolatry, God says, "Remember the sabbath day" (Exodus 20:8). The Creator had a deeper purpose in mind here than the casual holiday we have allowed Sunday to become.

In 587 B.C. Nebuchadnezzar destroyed the temple of Jerusalem. Jewish leaders were carried off as slaves to Babylon.

Like the ten northern tribes which had been destroyed a hundred years earlier, the tribe of Judah had little chance to survive. But *they kept the sabbath*. Every week for generations, the rabbi called them together to remember their covenant and to worship God. In worship, they maintained their identity.

Later, upon returning to Jerusalem, they realized that all the while they thought of themselves as keeping the sabbath, in fact *the sabbath was keeping them*. Even in captivity they remembered who they were and turned aside to get in tune with God.

I heard of the mountaineer who wrote a letter to a radio station. "I live up here on this mountain alone. All I have is a banjo to entertain myself. But my banjo is out of tune. I can hardly play it. If you on the radio would play for me an 'A-440' I could tune up my banjo."

The station manager laughed at first. Then he thought "What a human interest story." So three days in a row, at the agreed time, they broadcast an A-440 so an old mountaineer could tune up his banjo.

To me, that's what Sunday is all about. It's a time in the midst of all my busyness in which I can come and retune myself to God. Sunday, like an oasis in the desert, keeps me from perishing on my life's journey.

Sunday offers me a special time to worship, study, rest, and serve God.

1. *On Sunday I worship.*[1]

Worship reigns as the most important activity I do. It keeps me in touch with God.

My faith is so fragile that sometimes I don't remember God. Like George, my mind gets caught up in a million other things. Yet, from time to time, I experience God really present with me for a moment.

These unique experiences happen to me most often during

[1] I know that the sabbath was the seventh day, which is technically Saturday. I also know that the early church shifted the day of rest and worship to Sunday, the first day of the week, primarily because of the resurrection on the first day of the week. It's not my purpose to argue for or against which is the proper day. Therefore, I use the sabbath and Sunday interchangeably.

a formal Sunday morning worship service. It may be during
the singing of a hymn, or some phrase sung by the choir, an
idea from the sermon, or a random thought during the morning
prayer. Suddenly I feel that God wraps his arms around me,
calls me by name, and promises that all will be okay, because
he is God. In such a moment I worship. I don't keep those
moments. They get away from me and my mind returns to
lesser thoughts.

Those split seconds of faith, when I worship, mean more
to me than all the rest of the week. Those *kairos* moments
give meaning to my life. Without them I simply grow older
every day and, too soon, I die. Worship reminds me that God
holds my life secure, both now and forever.

Worship distinguishes me from animals. The horse is faster,
the elephant bigger, the mosquito more prolific, and the but-
terfly is far more beautiful. But I worship and when I do, I
feel only a "little less than God" (Psalm 8:5).

Several years ago Atlanta woke up to a world covered with
ice and snow. It was Sunday morning so I bundled up and
trudged out to the church. If anyone showed up, I wanted to
be there. At eleven o'clock I stood alone in the sanctuary.
Suddenly the thought hit me that we had scheduled this time
and place for the worship of God. I was the only one there so
I did it all. I followed the bulletin and performed every element
in the order of worship. To be honest, I skipped the sermon
but that was all. I prayed out loud, sang the hymns, and even
gave my offering. That morning proved to be one of the unique
worship experiences of my life. I felt God's presence with me
in a way so strong that I will carry its memory with me for
the rest of my life. It was a "burning bush" to me.

2. *On Sunday I study.*

Some say God's most valuable investment in us is the gift
of a sound mind. I agree. When I look into the eyes of a child
and see the spark of bright sanity there, I feel gratitude. The
ability to think is not a right that we humans can take for
granted, but a gift.

Perhaps I'm sensitive to this because my son is retarded. Most of the time Gene struggles with frustration and confusion. As I watch him with the appearance of a man and the mind of a child, I wonder if God sees me that way. Do I stumble around like a clumsy child in God's sight because I am too busy to overcome my ignorance? Do I have a right to go through life on a sixth-grade level simply because most television programming aims at that level? Or do I have a responsibility to use my mind to its highest potential?

If I don't take time to study, my mind will become lazy and go to seed. Sunday gives me a break in the week's routine so I can read without neglecting other responsibilities. I owe it to God to study the Bible and I owe it to others to know how they interpret it. Most of all, I owe it to myself to know what I can believe about God and what God expects of me. Whatever the price I must pay to study,. I am willing to pay it in order to wrap my mind around this tremendous idea that God loves me and has a plan for my life. So, I set aside time to read about the experiences others have had with God and how they understand God.

3. *On Sunday I rest.*

Sometimes I feel that I also lead a double life. There are two of me and I run so fast that I leave a part of me behind.

I remember flying home from overseas. My body landed in this city, but emotionally I was left behind across the ocean. I felt it would take at least a week for my feeling-self to catch up with the rest of me.

This split-person feeling overtakes me when I get tired and have too much to do. Then comes Sunday.

I use Sunday to get myself together. I stop running long enough to catch up with myself.

I put my body to bed. Only an emergency or an unusually important responsibility will interfere with my Sunday afternoon nap time. I remember announcing to a brunch group, "I'm sorry that I have to leave, but I have a very important nap to take." There is no way to measure the frayed nerves and careless mistakes I make when I don't "catch up on my rest" once a week.

It feels as if the energy I expend in one day never fully replaces itself in one night's sleep. Each succeeding day draws on my reserve until I can slow down on Sunday. Work seven days a week for long and I get sick.

Experts tell us that more than half of the hospital beds in America are filled by people with nonphysical illnesses. Our Creator showed knowledge of our needs by setting aside one day in every week and saying, "In it you shall not do any work" (Exodus 20:10).

Of course, rest comes in many forms. A first-century slave needed the command to do no labor. On that day he allowed his body to take it easy and muscles to relax.

On the other hand, many people today work more with their brains than with their muscles. A game of golf or a long walk may be more restful than taking a nap. When I concentrate all week long on a specific problem, the last thing I want to do is lie in a hammock all day. My body stops but my mind keeps on working.

Whatever it takes to recreate myself emotionally, spiritually, and physically receives high priority in my Sunday schedule.

4. *On Sunday I serve.*

Jesus did works of mercy on Sunday. He healed the man with a paralyzed hand on the sabbath day. To Jesus, the most sacred time was that used for helping a person in need.

There can be no adequate time for God that does not include service to others.

I seek to serve God in three ways.

First, I serve through the church. The church cannot survive without the volunteer labor and leadership of people giving time for God. In the congregation I serve, 116 groups meet on a regular basis for study, service, and fellowship. All of these groups depend upon volunteers to lead and support them. I make myself available to carry part of that load.

I serve because the church needs it, but I serve mainly

because I need to do it. I benefit more than those to whom my efforts are directed.

I remember Carolyn's words after she had given a pint of blood. "I feel fine. In fact, I've never felt better in my life." I watched the eyes of those who had taken time to give blood, for someone they would never meet, and their faces radiated with joy. This same enthusiasm for life can be experienced by those who teach Sunday church school, sing in the choir, or help cut the church grass.

In addition to the good feelings which accompany my service, I enjoy the fellowship of others who serve. Those who work together toward a common good inevitably develop a love for one another. Two of the closest friends I know met each other digging a ditch in the church yard; one was a banker, the other an engineer. They have been friends now for twelve years. The rewards of giving time for God last for a lifetime.

Second, I serve God by personal involvement with those in need.

I visit those who are sick, write thank-you letters, and take time to sit down and talk with children. My most rewarding involvement grew out of a visit to a needy family.

One day I drove down Main Street, turned off on to a lesser road, then a gravel road. Finally, at the end of a dirt road I entered a broken-down shack crowded with a family living hardly better than animals. Before I could sit down, they offered me something to eat. For an hour I listened to their struggles as they shared problems. "Even if you can't help us," the mother said, "we thank you for caring."

I was able to help. A week later I helped their oldest son find a job. I have never forgotten it and neither has he. I still hear from him occasionally with reports of success and gratitude. If my life holds no other value, I can at least look at some others I have helped along the way.

Third, I serve God by giving money.

Every dollar I donate represents a slice of my life. So much time, talent, and energy went into producing a dollar. When

I give it for a godly cause, I give a part of me.

However, I don't worship, study, rest, and serve only on Sundays. I schedule these times with God all through the week.

I chose Sunday as my example because I have noticed that those who rush through this day without giving it to God seldom, if ever, find time for God. Those who honor this day usually set aside many times for God all through the week.

Of course many people have to work on weekends and can't reserve the traditional day of Sunday as their special time. Many of them choose other times to worship, study, rest, and serve God. The important thing is not *which* day but rather that *some* day be set aside. It helps me to keep open to my personal need to include God in my daily life.

It's so important for me to keep my relationship with God in proper order. I don't keep Sunday *in order that* God will love me, I seek time for God in my life *because* God loves me. I don't make time for God because *God* needs it but because *I* do. I don't carry God, God carries me.

To some people, including George, religion becomes a heavy load. Church, God, and doctrine weigh heavy like burdens. "It's hardly worth the struggle," they say. But those who think of God as a burden to be carried need to take another look.

The Babylonians carried their gods. Isaiah watched them hoist Bel and Nebo upon their heads and ceremoniously cart them into battle. Yet, if things went bad for them, if it looked as though they might lose, they bowed their backs, dragged their noses in the dust, and carried their gods like dumb animals to a safe refuge. Isaiah laughed.

"Hearken to me, O house of Jacob . . . who have been borne by me from your birth, carried from the womb; even to your old age I am He, and to gray hairs I will carry you. I have made, and I will bear; I will carry and will save" (Isaiah 46:3-4). God never has to come to us to *be carried*. God carries us.

Later, Jesus read, "Come to me, all who labor and are heavy laden, and I will give you rest" (Matthew 11:28).

Did Jesus mean that he would free us of all burdens? If so, "Get out the hammock. If there's anything I need, it's rest, I'm coming to Jesus," I once said. But the call to rest is not an invitation to lie down and sleep.

Jesus adds, "Take my yoke upon you . . ." (Matthew 11:29).

Is the call to rest a call to commitment? Sounds like New Testament double-talk.

Jesus explains. "For my yoke is easy, and my burden is light" (Matthew 11:30). The clue to his promise lies in the word yoke, which is a device worn on the shoulder by which we can carry a burden which otherwise would crush us.

We don't go through life burden-free, but we can choose our load. "Take *my* yoke," Jesus said.

Because his yoke fits.

Envision this scene at Jesus' carpenter shop. Many a farmer came to the young Jesus. "Look at this poor beast. His neck is chafed, he can't work."

Jesus would lift the yoke from the animal, sand and reshape the yoke until it formed a smooth fit. Then the ox could plow without pain. Jesus feels the same concern for us when the yoke doesn't fit. We carry burdens in life that God never intended that we carry.

Someone said, "I spend money I don't have, to buy things I don't need, because of advertising I don't believe, to impress neighbors I don't even like." That may be a bit flippant but it speaks the truth for many of us. How often do we spend our days doing things which hold no lasting meaning, until we are worn out for nothing?

The yoke of Christ which I have described as worship, study, rest, and service strengthens us to carry the other loads of life. His yoke fits. We were created to worship and serve God.

Also, the yoke joins two animals together in pulling a load.

In the same way, the yoke of Christ binds us to him. He even carries the heavier end.

Five-year-old David picked up a suitcase weighing half as much as he and measuring half as tall.

"That's too heavy for you, son."

"I carry it, Daddy," he proudly responded. Halfway to the car, David gave out. He sat down by the suitcase.

"Well, what are you going to do now?" Dad asked.

"You made me, Daddy, you carry me."

In the same way, God carries me when the load of life gets too heavy. But I can forget and try to carry it all alone. That's why I take time for God, to remember that God made me and God will carry me.

Postscript

I attended George's funeral today.

As I reflect on his life, I realize how much I am like him. George represents the other side of my personality. All the success, pressures, and insecurities that drove him, push me, too. The only difference is that I push back two ways.

Rather than trying to get more done in less time, I seek for more time in which to do less.

Also, *at the end of a period of time, rather than looking at what I have accomplished, I want to know what I have become.*

I see this life as a short moment in a long process of a more abundant life. Compared to eternity, this life is but a handsbreadth.

I read of a clock in the physics lab at Johns Hopkins University that measures time down to a *trillionth* of a second. To help us visualize something so short, they explain that's "about the time it would take a ray of light traveling at the rate of 186,000 miles per second to go the distance measured by the thickness of one playing card."[1]

When I realize the brevity of these days here, it causes me to ease up, to accept my limitations and place great value on quality time. I vow that I will never again allow those things

[1] Edward T. Hall, *Dance of Life* (New York: Doubleday & Co., Inc., 1983), p. 21.

that matter the least to crowd out those things that matter the most. I will seek *kairos* time.

When the day comes that I join George on the other side of this life, I believe I will gain a new perspective on time.

First, eternity will be point time and not linear.

In this life I see time as a string. It stretches out behind me and I measure its length and compare its highs and lows. Unfortunately the string of time stops or turns the corner at the present moment. I cannot see what is stretched out ahead. The future remains unknown. Therefore, how I choose to live in the eternal present is determined more by my poorly remembered past than by the unknown future into which I am moving. In eternity the present perspective reverses.

With God, and with us from the moment we pass from this world of space and time, time as we now know it will be no more. "For a thousand years in thy sight are but as yesterday when it is past" (Psalm 90:4). God sees time as a point. He takes the string of time and rolls it up into an infinitesimal ball and sees it all at once: past, present, and future. Life will take on new dimensions for we shall see it all as it is . . . in a moment . . . without anxiety.

Second, in eternity, *chronos* time will be totally absorbed in *kairos*. Life will be pure quality.

Jesus faced the other side with a promise on his lips. "Paradise." Whatever else that word means, it emphasizes quality, God-filled, meaningful time.

All of this will be mine, not because I earned it or won the race, but because God chooses for me to have it. God promises to be on my side.

I am reminded of the Little Leaguer's dad who was pressed into serving as a third-base umpire. He had never done anything like this before, but the official umpire failed to show up. Either he called the plays at third base or the game had to be postponed. Even though his own son played on one of the teams, he agreed. The game started. His son came to bat. Immediately this father-umpire heard a heckler in the stands behind.

"What?" yelled the heckler. "He's too little to play on this team. Get him a girl's uniform."

The son struck out.

Three innings later the umpire's son came to the plate again.

"Easy out," the heckler cried, even louder. "Just roll the ball to him."

Again the boy struck out.

Then next time, with the heckler yelling every insult he could think of, the nine-year-old batter drove the ball all the way to the fence. Grinning from ear to ear, he rounded first, touched second, and ran with all his might toward third. "Slide," yelled the coach, but he was tagged out two feet from the bag.

"Safe!" yelled the umpire.

With that, the heckler ran down into the field screaming. "Safe? Why he was out by a mile."

Dad stood there but said nothing.

"What kind of an umpire are you anyhow?" the heckler demanded.

"Not a very good one," the umpire responded. "But I'm one heck of a Dad."

I recognize the breakdown of this analogy if pushed too far. But *I believe this is the way God is with me.*

God calls me "safe," not because I outrun anyone else or get there first. God calls me safe because God is my Creator and I'm God's child and we have all eternity together.

So what's my rush?

Suggestions for
Further Reading

Bauman, Edward, *et al., The Holistic Health Lifebook.* comp. Berkeley Holistic Health Center. San Francisco: And/Or Press, 1981.

Culligan, Matthew J., and Sedlocek, Keith, *How to Kill Stress Before It Kills You.* New York: Gramercy Publishing Co., 1976.

Dunbar, Flanders, *Mind and Body: Psychosomatic Medicine.* New York: Random House, 1947.

Freudenberger, Herbert, and Richelson, Geraldine, *Burn-Out: The Melancholia of High Achievement.* New York: Doubleday & Co., Inc., 1980.

Friedman, Meyer, and Rosenman, Ray H., *Type A Behavior and Your Heart.* New York: Alfred A. Knopf, Inc., 1974.

Girdano, Daniel A., and Everly, George S., Jr., *Controlling Stress and Tension: A Holistic Approach.* Englewood Cliffs, N.J.: Prentice Hall, Inc., 1979.

Goldberg, Philip, *Executive Health.* New York: McGraw-Hill Publishing Co., 1979.

Hall, Edward T., *Dance of Life: The Other Dimension of Time.* New York: Doubleday & Co., Inc., 1983.

Kennedy, Eugene, *A Time for Being Human*. New York: Simon & Schuster, Inc., 1978.

Kostyu, Frank A., *The Time of Your Life Is Now*. New York: Seabury Press, Inc., 1977.

Lair, Jess, *I Ain't Much Baby——But I'm All I've Got*. Center City, Minn.: Hazelden Foundation, 1969.

————, *I Ain't Well——But I Sure Am Better*. Center City, Minn.: Hazelden Foundation, 1975.

Lakein, Alan, *How to Get Control of Your Time and Your Life*. New York: The New American Library Inc., 1974.

Leas, Speed B., *Time Management*. Creative Leadership Series, ed. Lyle E. Schaller. Nashville: Abingdon Press, 1978.

Levi, Lennart, *Stress: Sources, Management, and Prevention*. New York: Liveright, 1967.

McQuade, Walter, and Aikman, Ann, *Stress*. New York: Bantam Books, Inc., 1975.

Mackenzie, R. Alec, *The Time Trap*. New York: Amacon, A division of American Management Associations, 1972.

May, Rollo, *The Meaning of Anxiety*. New York: Simon & Schuster, 1979.

Mills, James W., *Coping with Stress: A Guide to Living*. New York: John Wiley & Sons, Inc., 1982.

Rassieur, Charles L., *Stress Management for Ministers*. Philadelphia: The Westminster Press, 1982.

Rubin, Theodore Isaac, *Angry Book*. New York: Macmillan Publishing Co., Inc., 1970.

Scott, Dru, *How to Put More Time in Your Life*. New York: Rawson Wade, 1980.

Sehnert, Keith W., *Stress-Unstress*. Minneapolis: Augsburg Publishing House, 1981.

Selye, Hans, *The Stress of Life*. New York: Bantam Books, Inc., 1976.

Shedd, Charlie W., *Time for All Things*. Nashville: Abingdon Press, 1980.

Simonton, Carl, *et al.*, *Getting Well Again*. New York: Bantam Books, Inc., 1980.

Smith, Donald P., *Clergy in the Cross Fire: Coping With Conflicts in the Ministry*. Philadelphia: The Westminster Press, 1974.